D1003955

ANSWERING EVIL

CRISIS, COMPASSION AND TRUTH IN

AN AGE OF UNCERTAINTY

— EXPANDED EDITION —

JAY McCARL

ANSWERING EVIL: EXPANDED EDITION
CRISIS, COMPASSION AND TRUTH IN AN AGE OF
UNCERTAINTY

BY JAY RICHARD MCCARL

Second Edition, Revised
Copyright © 2015 Jay Richard McCarl
Revised 2019

BIBLICAL DINNERS MINISTRIES
P.O. Box 111, Greenwood, CA 95635-0111
Website: BiblicalDinners.com
E-Mail: Jay@BiblicalDinners.org

No portion of this book may be reproduced, stored in a retrieval system, or transmitted in any form or by any means without prior written permission from the author.

All Scripture quotations, unless otherwise indicated, are taken from the HOLY BIBLE, NEW INTERNATIONAL VERSION®. NIV®. Copyright © 1973, 1978, 1984 by International Bible Society. Used by permission of Zondervan. All rights reserved.

For the giants
on whose shoulders I stood to write this,
especially Os Guinness, Gayle Erwin
and Mark O'Sullivan,
whose wisdom revealed an unexpected world…

…and for my wife Kathee
who, despite her petite elegance,
has the broadest shoulders of all

CONTENTS

.

Roadmap
Through the Badlands

Evil and suffering can be answered—and although the answers are not exactly the ones most people are looking for, they are perfect, and they are big. But to get there, our journey must begin on solid ground, and that means we have to drain a philosophical swamp. The first part of this book cuts a path through that swamp. Next, the trail plunges headlong into a battleground of religious ideas that are, in our age of unbridled tolerance, neither politically nor religiously correct. And then the road narrows. A lot.

We will pass by relics and ruins of history and ideas—ill-served events and characters dotting an endless, one-dimensional line. But history and ideas illuminate when viewed through a great wide-angle lens instead of the pinched eyepiece of a microscope. They are the sun and stars shining out of a vast universe stretched over continents and time—a world flowing with multi-dimensional currents and movements of thought that filled epochs and empires.

Evil and suffering are fused to that landscape and they must be viewed the same way if any sense is to be made of them at all, much less answers. Looking through that broad lens, the terrain often becomes *more* distinct, not less. If we strain at the pebbles on the path, we may miss the sunrise...

Blessings.

Jay McCarl

Part One

READY OR NOT...

"You have a problem with authority, Mr. Anderson. You believe you are special, that somehow the rules do not apply to you. Obviously, you are mistaken."

—Mr. Rhineheart, *The Matrix*

THE RHINOCEROS

"I used to think a crisis was when Bertha got
skipped on the prayer chain."

—Law Enforcement Chaplain Scott Hubbard

"Jay, I need you to stand-by for a death notification," my supervising chaplain alerted me, "It's going to be in your neighborhood." Then, in a flat, matter-of-fact tone, he told me who it was. The woman killed by the drunk driver was the lovely young wife of a close friend. It was the second most painful notification I ever made.

I was now in a race to track down my friend before some well-meaning bystander contacted him first and ruined his life with unofficial information. At least I would ruin it with the facts. Forty heart-pounding minutes later I found him at a home Bible study, just a few doors away from his house.

Knock knock knock knock knock...

A middle-aged man wearing tan trousers and a Hawaiian

shirt opened the door, flooding the front porch with a cheerful light. He recognized me and invited inside, where my searching gaze was met by a dozen familiar, smiling faces looking up from their Bibles—including that of my friend.

"Come with me," I said and ushered him into a back bedroom. The men in the living room stopped smiling. I was in uniform.

We sat on the shoulder of an unmade bed. It was warm and comfortable. And then I told him.

Without a word he rose, bolted past the men and out the front door. He was going home. I struggled to keep up with his frantic pace, and a ringing started in my head that swelled into a scream, grating against the silence. It was going to be a long night for everyone.

Two of the Bible study leaders followed close behind, and when they reached my friend's door, I pulled them in and put them to work. They were respected elders at their church, but with an event of this magnitude, they were dismayed and clueless.

"Just sit with him, hold his hand and pray," I said to one, "We will need glasses of water and tissues," I told the other. I took a deep breath and closed my eyes as I ran down my mental list of death notification procedures. "What next?" I asked myself. *Call his pastor.*

He was an ordained minister who served nearly sixty years in the pulpit—he was tall, noble and wizened, and within minutes he was knocking at the door. He greeted me cordially, but his eyes were dark and tentative, his face furrowed with age and deep concern. He shook my hand. "Good evening, chaplain. What do you want me to do?" he asked softly. This was an obvious question, as the dynamics of such a tragedy are extremely fluid. "The husband is in the living room and things are relatively under control. You can go in and talk to him."

"Thank you," the minister replied, still clasping my hand, "But what do you want me to *do*?" I blinked, puzzled by his repetition of the question until it struck me that *he didn't really know what to do in the midst of such extreme circumstances*. The elderly pastor was a seasoned seminarian that had been in full-time ministry longer than I had been alive. Yet it seemed that no one ever showed him how to address the human and spiritual impact of a sudden catastrophe beyond the usual bouquet of Christian clichés and platitudes. *He wasn't sure how to answer such an immediate and searing level of pain.*

And this may be the most troubling void in the experience of those who want to help and those who are supposed to.

What do I say? What do I do? Who am I to be to my shattered friend?

Every one of us lives in a sunny world of gardens blooming with goodness and beauty. This is the world of wishes—the world of our dreams. But that same sunny world has a dark habit of turning real, erupting into tragedy. We love the thought of walking hand in hand under the dazzling blue sky of a romantic tropical beach, but most of us are woefully unprepared to walk hand in hand with a friend through the valley of the shadow of death. We are full of ready answers to happiness and peace—musings dripping with sentiments and smiles. But how do we answer evil when it strikes? And it will.

As compassionate beings made in God's likeness, it makes sense that we should all possess answers to evil and suffering, especially those of us who serve in some form of ministry. We, perhaps more than others, are expected to hold a quality of compassion that reaches beyond predictable spiritual clichés. But when I became a law enforcement chaplain, I was stunned to find that most people—and most ministers, regardless of their educational or denominational background—or even experience— knew little or nothing of how to deal with people reeling from the impact of sudden extreme crisis.

And most people *still* don't know. Colleges, universities, seminaries and divinity schools offer students plenty of theological discussion *about* evil and suffering, but little is taught about how to look it in the eye and do something about it. And this is a grave oversight, considering that compassion, grace and mercy are the bedrock of our Christian duty.

It's true that we may never know this side of heaven what God *intended* by allowing a terrible tragedy to occur. But if truth exists with God, and if He has revealed His truth to us both in writing and in person, then an examination of what He said and did should tell us something of the *why* of evil and suffering. And it does. Even more, flowing from these revelations is a fountain of compassion that cushions evil's impact and lightens its malignant aftereffects.

We *need* to know this. It is the substance of the Truth we can offer others—and all the more because *others* will inevitably need it, too. It is not about answering the dark evil of demonic forces (which is a different discussion), but rather the crushing questions of tragedies and tumults common to all of us who live in this fallen world.

There are no pat answers, and the mental gymnastics of philosophies are helpless to alleviate the pain of grief. The problem of evil and suffering, however, is still the rhinoceros in our china shop, and despite all the enlightened discussion about it, it snorts and defiantly refuses to leave.

So we must face the beast on his own ground—not in lofty towers where deep thinkers hammer away at the brute, but in tear-soaked living rooms and at roadside wrecks. It is in ordinary places where the monster mocks all philosophical rhetoric.

"Is evil really real?" an armchair professor scoffs.

"And who is to say that bad is actually *bad*?" boasts another.

"Is suffering natural, supernatural, or is it just an irrational response to physical pain?" quibbles the relativist.

And on it goes. Yet such questions must be challenged, because, to the caregiver, neglecting them is to run naked onto the battlefield.

Even more—what about all the radically different worldviews of evil and suffering? For billions of people answers are revealed through the lens of religion, while for others it is merely a matter of being rational about things. But to what end? Does religion provide answers to evil? Does rationalism? Can either wipe tears from the faces of the miserable? And perhaps most important of all, does any system or faith possess the authority to offer more than milky platitudes for suffering and death?

Can there be meaning and purpose in our pain?

Can there be *truth* in it?

ANSWERING FOR GOD

"But the fight for our planet, physical and spiritual, a fight of cosmic proportions, is not a vague matter of the future; it has already started. The forces of Evil have begun their decisive offensive, you can feel their pressure, and yet your screens and publications are full of prescribed smiles and raised glasses. What is the joy about?"

—Alexander Solzhenitsyn

"Evil and suffering are so nearly universal as to underscore how vulnerable we all are as humans and what it means that we are mortal…"

—Os Guinness

It *will* happen. The phone will ring at midnight, or a loud desperate pounding at your door will startle you awake at three in the morning. Something has happened to someone, and at that hour of night it is *never* good news.

You don't have to be in ministry to get dragged out of bed or pulled away from a meal to comfort someone battered by the storms of a relentless world. In fact, you will. You will be conscripted to toil in the eye of a raging emotional hurricane, comforting crushed souls desperate to escape the onslaught of evil and suffering. But you are only in the *eye* of the hurricane—and though the worst part of the storm seems to have blown past, the most destructive blast of the tempest is rapidly approaching.

There in the ruins before you reel human beings—stunned, numb and astonished. Their minds are helpless to grasp the terrible thing that just happened, that it was *real* and that it happened to *them*. And whether or not they know it, they have great need of your presence, because you are the presence of Christ. They need your touch, because it is the warmth of God's hand. But most of all they cry out for answers that will bring meaning and purpose to their torment. They want to know *why*. Through tears and clenched teeth they clamber for reasons to the nightmare they are forced to endure, and now that you have come, they expect *you* to answer for God.

But how do you do that? Helpers struggle to recall sayings and clever quotes coined to appease the huge questions posed by evil and suffering, and when offered, apologize for their inadequacy. Many wise men have lamented that there are few (if any) real answers, and that pursuing the *why* is futile and beyond finding out. Others insist that evil *must* have its way, that terror and trauma are mysterious tactics of God's will. They sigh with resignation and in hushed tones explain that all answers to human tragedy lie veiled in the mind of the Almighty, infinitely beyond the reach of our vulgar understanding.

But clever sayings ring with hollow compassion. They are stinging words poured into open wounds—platitudes that are not only useless, but also dishonest. No one knows this more than a victim. Grief-stricken people grasp for substance. They ransack their private storehouse of clichés, snatching up every sentiment and superstitious incantation to assuage the pain. In their agony, they somehow know that a good answer brings more healing than the best doctor.

And real answers exist. Truthful answers. And they have been put on display in plain view. In fact, God intends such answers, *His* answers, to be seen and understood as if suffering people everywhere were entitled to them. And they are.

This demands that we need to know what we're talking about—to be able to speak about it to people desperate for a soft pillow on which to lay a weary heart.

This is easy to say but hard to do. Answering evil has been the philosophical irritant of history, the gargoyle of human thought—defying reason and logic when tragedy strikes. And it has provoked some of life's most disturbing questions:

> *If God is benevolent—if He is all powerful, all knowing, able to do anything—if He truly loves—then why does He allow, perhaps cause, His own children to suffer agony,*

cruelty, destruction, chaos, terror, death, and worse?

How can catastrophes like war, torture, genocide and massive human loss continue under His loving, watchful eye without holy outrage and miraculous intervention on behalf of the downtrodden?

Why does His fierce vengeance not rain down upon the cruel oppressor?

If He is omnipotent, why does He not move the very heavens to foil the forces laying waste to His beloved humanity?

Is He even there?

If He is, would He not be the devil?

These are the cries of anguished hearts—the wreckage left behind by the storm—and magic words will never budge a crushing slab of doubt. Pry-bars are needed—iron words of real truth that can free the victim. A soft pillow is needed, too—grace for a tired heart that will allow it to breathe deeply and rest.

Have you noticed that when the sky falls, the crushed and broken tend to gravitate toward the man or woman of God— toward *you*? You are the one they expect to carry such mighty equipment.

"Answer for your God," they plead, for in the mind of the victim, if not you, then who?

Part Two

DEFINING EVIL

"Now the LORD God had planted a garden in the east, in Eden; and there he put the man he had formed. And the LORD God made all kinds of trees grow out of the ground—trees that were pleasing to the eye and good for food. In the middle of the garden were the tree of life and the tree of the knowledge of good and evil."

—Genesis 2:8-9

"Understanding does not cure evil, but it is a definite help, inasmuch as one can cope with a comprehensible darkness."

—Carl Jung

RELENTLESS REALITY

EVIL | ˈēvəl|, noun:

1. the fact of suffering, misfortune, and wrongdoing
2. a cosmic evil force
3. something that brings sorrow, distress, or calamity

—Merriam-Webster's Collegiate Dictionary

If evil is a myth, then so is God—if evil exists, then so does God.

Strange, isn't it?

Now, stay with me on this. Such declarations about God and evil are increasingly rebuked as foolishness. The bulk of modern thinking insists that God is an opinion or at least irrelevant. This is the bent of modern Rationalism. "Reason is the supreme authority in all matters of knowledge, opinion, belief and conduct," it boasts, "and unaided by God, it will be our guide in all truth."

Rationalism is a powerful idea, but like religion, which it seeks to marginalize, it is still a *belief.* According to its tenets, recognizing the existence of a fixed standard of evil would be nothing short of intellectual suicide. In Rationalism, for evil to *objectively* be called evil, you would also have to bow to the reality of an objective Standard-Setter. *God.* But the mere suggestion of His existence upsets the whole reason for *reason* by tossing faith into the equation. This forces a theological question that Rationalism rejects as irrational (and in all likelihood, insulting). So, for the Rationalist, a thing is evil not because God makes the rules, but *because I say it is.*

But what if someone else says differently?

Never mind that—it's what I believe.

In a faith where people worship reason as supreme master and guide, evil could never be defined except in the imagination of each individual. And that's a real problem. Evil could be neither bad nor wrong because an absolute definition of anything would be impossible, making each person's own private interpretation of evil and suffering meaningless to everyone else (and to the whole universe, for that matter).

But Rationalism is right about one thing: evil cannot be a real thing apart from the existence of an actual, self-existent, objective, sovereign God. In fact, to define evil at all, an unchanging standard of absolute goodness must exist, must be revealed, and must somehow possess a nonnegotiable authority. For evil to be *evil*, it must be viewed through a sovereign lens, which would harden its definition into a fixed category of its own.

In other words, though there may be countless torments and degrees of evil suffered by people, evil would still be *evil* and could never be seen as good or even undecided. *Ever.* The definition of evil *as evil* is entirely dependent upon the existence of a God who made all the rules.

On the other hand, if God is only a myth, then for us humans pleasure becomes the measure of all things good or bad because we can experience it apart from any belief in a Supreme Being. Life, however, has a funny way of reminding us that it is not made up of pleasures. In fact, mankind's relentless pursuit of it proves that pleasure is an annoyingly elusive prey.

Humanity, according to Rationalism, evolved accidentally on a remote planet adrift in a dangerous universe that never had us in mind. This is an unsettling idea. For any creature with nerves and a brain living in such a random place, physical discomfort is the order of the day, every day. But unlike animals, we humans are self-aware—and our *awareness* of our precarious place in the cosmos reveals something irrational in us: an irresistible yearning to assign moral values to pleasure, peril and pain.

For instance, if something gives you pleasure then it must be good because it makes you feel good. But if something causes you pain, what is it that makes it *bad?* In a rational universe it would simply be the biological response of nature strumming on your nerves and would be neither good nor bad. The level of your neurological discomfort could measure the intensity of your suffering and pain, but it would not give it any meaning. And for us humans, these mechanics of nature have never been adequate to answer the feelings of *badness* of something that hurts.

And that's the problem. We humans desire pleasure, and we almost never question (or even consider) the meaning of a happy experience when we are caught up in the moment. But is our experience good because it is an agreeable physical response or because it is *good*? *Good* is a moral measure. But pleasure fades and unpleasurable things happen—and when they do, it not only produces physical sensations that are contrary to pleasure and well-being, it triggers outrage that provokes people to demand the meaning behind it. *Unpleasurable* becomes *bad,* and *bad* quickly becomes *evil*. You can tell the instant you hear a victim scream, "Why???"

Can "bad" be defined merely as whatever interferes with our pleasure or its pursuit? Pleasure can and does occur naturally—but how is it "good" without introducing a standard of "badness" into the equation by which we can measure pleasure? Further, in an accidental universe that never had us in mind, how can we refer to "badness" as "bad" other than by some fleeting perception of it? And where did we get such a notion?

If evil is a myth, then so is God; if evil exists, then so does God.

THE RHETORIC OF "WHY?"

"My argument against God was that the universe seemed so cruel and unjust. But how had I got this idea of just and unjust? A man does not call a line crooked unless he has some idea of a straight line."

—C.S. Lewis

It's only a matter of time. Every human life, including your own, will eventually be upended by a "bad" event. But when it happens, the questions that tear at our minds will be far more troubling than our own hardnosed objections to the circumstances. People charge that they are victims of *injustice*—and you can tell just by listening to them. "Why me?" they cry, thrusting empty hands toward the heavens.

Almost anyone can study the facts of a bad event and understand (to a certain extent) the mechanics of the situation. But people everywhere and from every age of history have proven that the *how* of a tragedy matters little compared to the *why*. They are not pleading for an explanation, but for a *just* explanation of what happened, for the *reason* for the bad thing. "Why did it happen to *me*, and not someone else?" "Why should it happen to me at all?" "What did I do to deserve *this*?"

Even philosophers have occasionally tipped their hand with their own pained cries, revealing a sense of justice lurking in the shadows of their great rational minds. C.S. Lewis reasoned,

> "My argument against God was that the universe seemed so cruel and unjust. But how had I got this idea of just and unjust? A man does not call a line crooked unless he has some idea of a straight line…If the whole universe has no meaning, we should never have found out that it has no meaning: just as, if there were no light in the universe and therefore no creatures with eyes, we should never know it was dark. Dark would be a word without meaning."[i]

The demand for the "why" of a tragedy is not only common to all of us, it is normal. Even more, it reveals an unrelenting sense of justice that insists that the bad thing is somehow grossly unfair and out of balance. And most interesting of all, even atheists and rationalists—wittingly or unwittingly—lash out with the same cry.

But a pained "why" from the mouth of an avowed rationalist—much less an atheist—signals a tremendous leap of illogic. It is the plea of a tormented man crying out to a dark, impersonal universe to judge between the weight of the good he has done versus what has happened to him. Who do they think will answer? Why do they ask at all?

The idea that pain is painful because it irritates the human neurological system should more than satisfy the cool logic of any rationalist, but it never does. It is not just that a tragedy happened, but that it happened to *me*, and it is somehow *unfair*. But to reject an objective, measurable standard of fairness (i.e., the dictates of a sovereign God) makes the idea of justice meaningless. In a God-less universe "why me" makes no sense. Appealing for fairness counts for nothing in an arbitrary, unsympathetic cosmos, in which we are its random dust.

This is a huge problem. Justice and injustice are flights of fancy without some predefined basis of good and evil, yet all people everywhere possess an inborn sense of justice. But in the rationalist's universe good and evil are *not* reasonable, so labeling anything as "unjust" not only presumes the existence of *badness,* but badness as *bad*. And *that* is a standard of evil.

Let me put it another way: if we live in an arbitrary universe where unpleasant things just happen to people, nothing could be judged as either fair or unfair. But when unpleasant things happen to *me* or to others—things that are considered bad and irrational—why is it that we *don't* respond with indifference? We react—and harshly, with degrees of outrage. And our outrage not only points the finger at the injustice of the tragedy, but it exposes a knowledge of good and of evil residing deep within our human nature.

Interestingly, anger at injustice echoes the disastrous effect of the half-truth/whole-lie of Satan's deception in the Garden of Eden. The devil assured Eve that if she ate the fruit of a particular tree, her eyes would be opened and she would be like God, *knowing good and evil*. You probably know the rest of the story: she ate, and now we *all* know good and evil—and we never became gods. And now, because of our ill-gotten knowledge of good and evil, we also own a sense of real justice, which not only points to the existence of God, but in particular the God of the Bible (we will talk about this later). The fallout from this cataclysmic event explains the wrongness in the universe, the brokenness of the world, and humanity's natural bent towards evil—a condition which theologians have dubbed the "Fall of Man."

Our sense of justice is something that is deeply held by all people, including atheists and rationalists, and passionately so. And if this is not ironic enough, justice is rational and coherent only because it is deeply rooted in our innate discernment of good and evil. In fact, it appears that one cannot be reasonably understood apart from either.

CRUELTY

"I envied the arrogant when I saw the prosperity of
the wicked. They have no struggles; their bodies are
healthy and strong. They are free from the burdens
common to man; they are not plagued by human
ills.... Therefore their people turn to them and drink
up waters in abundance. They say, 'How can God
know? Does the Most High have knowledge?'"

—Asaph, Psalm 73:3-5, 10-11

The root of all human suffering draws from three main sources,
author and social critic Os Guinness suggests, and they are quite
obvious when you think about them: the vulnerability of the human
body, the devastating effects of nature and the infliction of
suffering and cruelty by others.[1] Nature inflicts upon our bodies its
share of suffering from disease, disasters, calamities and
catastrophes. But *people* have the capacity to be unspeakably cruel.

Both nature and human cruelty are common and deadly, yet

---

[1] As Guinness suggests, all three of these sources spring from the first, the
vulnerability of the human body.

they are often dream-like in the minds of the afflicted and unaffected alike. For instance, when someone cries out, "This can't be happening," or "This can't be happening *to me*," it reveals an irrational but very human denial of real suffering, as if it should not be happening at all. It seems that we are not, as one historian suggested, mere objects of nature among other objects.

It was Freud who coined the famous saying, "Life is hard to bear," referring to a condition that afflicted people with "a permanent state of anxious expectation." He may have been right.

Think about it: nature (in which we are immersed) and people (by whom we are surrounded) make suffering and cruelty a fearful inevitability for anyone with a human body. On the other hand, though people are fragile and vulnerable to the effects of evil, they tend to be both resilient and hopeful in their resistance of it, even in the face of impending death. This odd tension between fear and nobility is the fuel behind the idea of the evolutionary ascent of humanity. But in light of the devastating and ultimately fatal effects of nature and natural selection, stubborn human optimism is irrational—unless, of course, its source happens to be supernatural. Never were two worlds of thinking farther apart—yet like conjoined twins both the natural and supernatural are inseparably fused by our universal human response to suffering.

Horrific accidents, onslaughts of nature, wasting diseases and sudden, unanticipated losses of great magnitude conjure up frightening images of suffering like a monster that attacks in the dark and with indifference. Being battered by such a heartless brute provokes searing questions like "why *me*?" or "why did *this* have to happen?" But it happened anyway, and it hurts badly.

But other, more troubling questions boil in minds of the traumatized, questions demanding ultimate answers: Did *God* do this evil? If not, then why did He allow it to occur? Was this thing His will, and if so, why would He ever ordain such a monstrosity?

Now our sense of justice kicks in: most people will at least demand an answer from God as to what they did to deserve their pain. Others might turn against God and scorn Him for the evil that He inflicted or failed to prevent: God is mean. He is unjust. He is angry. He is punishing me. He is indifferent. God is against me. He must be on the side of my enemies. He could not possibly exist in the face of such pain and suffering. God is cruel. God is the devil.

It is here, amidst the turbulent accusations and logic of a man railing against his Maker that a great paradox suddenly comes to light. The anguished reasonings of a sufferer confirm humanity's inherent knowledge of the existence of a merciful and compassionate God who seems to be acting in a manner contrary to His loving nature.

Simply put, the reality of suffering does not verify the existence of an evil God, *but of an entirely good one.*

Villains and Villainy

Cruelty is different. It is unnatural. Its pain tears at the heart perhaps more than the body because there is a malevolent will behind it. Cruelty is deliberate; a wicked agony that feeds on tears and terror. It is dread laced with misery that poisons the hope of the helpless. It is the handiwork of a villain—someone cheerfully indifferent to human suffering. Yet here animosity against God becomes somewhat muted, because an act of cruelty is often seen as a *person* tormenting another person instead of God acting maliciously through accident or nature. Even so, the blame is loud.

For both the bystander and the tormented, cruelty generates turbulent and horrendously conflicted ideas about justice. This is especially true when it is happening to someone who is thought to be entirely unworthy of such malevolence—especially children. In his book, *The Future of an Illusion*, Sigmund Freud concluded that "There are the elements, which seem to mock at all human control: the earth... water... diseases... the painful riddle of death..."[ii] Seven years later, Freud admitted to an additional source of human suffering: *people*. He observed, "The suffering which comes from this last source is perhaps more painful to us than any other."[iii]

But even though our outrage is more focused on a human evildoer, God is not automatically exonerated. The difficulties are clear: Why would God allow the helpless and innocent to suffer at the hands of the cruel and guilty? Is God not just? Why then does the villain often thrive while the innocent suffer? Is God not outraged at cruelty and furious at the evildoer? Why does the all-judicious God not step in and rightly put an end to it?

Even more chilling: *what about the evildoer*? Were we not both villain and victim created in the image of God? If so, what does it reveal about God? Moreover, what does it reveal about the whole of humanity? And what does it reveal about *me*? Is not the evildoer a man *like me*, and am I not a man *like him*?

It was Holocaust survivor Primo Levy who, when he found himself unable to reconcile the cruelty and suffering in the world with the existence of a loving and benevolent God, coined the bitter and oft quoted phrase, "If there is an Auschwitz, then there cannot be a God."[iv] Forty-two years later he scrawled in pencil, "I find no solution to the riddle—I still seek and do not find it…" Not long after, he leapt down an open stairwell to his death. Unfortunately, like Primo Levy, many people who have also suffered great cruelty still believe in God enough to blame Him, but not enough to believe Him.

Part Three

A BLOT ON THE UNIVERSE

"Eager souls, mystics and revolutionaries, may propose to refashion the world in accordance with their dreams; but evil remains, and so long as it lurks in the secret places of the heart, utopia is only the shadow of a dream."

—Nathaniel Hawthorne

"What is evil? Whatever springs from weakness."

—Friedrich Nietzsche

"All evil—in fact the very existence of evil—is inexplicable until we refer to the paternity of God. It hangs a huge blot in the universe until the orb of divine love rises behind it. In that apposition we detect its meaning. It appears to us but a finite shadow as it passes across the disk of infinite light."

—Edwin Hubbell Chapin

NOT THE SAME

"All things are known by comparison, for comparison contains within itself a power which immediately demonstrates."

—Leon Battista Alberti

"We believe that all religions are basically the same—at least the one that we read was. They only differ on matters of creation, sin, heaven, hell, God and salvation."

—Steve Turner, British Journalist and Satirist

Author and lecturer Os Guinness wrote, "differences make a difference...not only for individuals but for whole societies and civilizations."[v]

In recent years it has become increasingly common to hear people declare, "All religions are basically the same," or, "We are all worshipping the same God." But no such declaration could be further from the truth. All you need to do is glance into the world's prevailing religious ideas and definitions of God, the origin of all things, the meaning of life, the universe, suffering and evil, to discover that they are all separated by vast and irreconcilable differences.

When we peel off the veneers of religious and political correctness, we find three distinct families of faith—all of which hold radically different ideas about evil and suffering. Dr. Guinness put it like this: First, there is the Eastern view, including the monumental religions of Hinduism and Buddhism, along with Confucianism, Daoism, Stoicism (included with the Eastern for reasons that I will address later) and various other New Age philosophies. Next is the secular view, which includes movements like secular humanism, atheism, rationalism, relativism and scientific dogmatism (sometimes referred to as "scientism"). Lastly, there is the Western view, consisting of the three great monotheistic religions of Christianity, Judaism, and Islam.[vi]

Since we navigate our lifeboats in the currents of religious diversity flowing through a rapidly evolving society, holding tightly to that which is true is non-negotiable. This is essential (as you will see later), not only for our own spiritual and emotional survival, but that we can also offer it for the healing of others—even when the dynamics of a particular crisis demand that many things go unspoken.

A *truthful* understanding of evil and suffering is *everything*—it slices through sentimental slush and baseless spirituality, providing fitting answers to religious devotees of all families of faith without compromising Biblical truth. The emphasis here is clearly on the Biblical view of evil and its origins, because no other family of faith has historically, philosophically or spiritually offered more substantial comfort and genuine hope for the casualties of life's most dreadful events.

THE EASTERN VIEW OF EVIL

"Who are you? Who am I? Wherefrom did I come? Who is my mother; who, my father? Think about them deeply and know that all experiences of the world are worthless dreams and give up on them…"

—Shankara

Row, row, row your boat, gently down the stream,
Merrily, merrily, merrily, merrily, life is but a dream.

—Traditional English Language Nursery Rhyme

Many of the great philosophies and religions of history were born out of a desperate plea for answers to evil and human suffering. Hinduism, Buddhism, Stoicism and various manifestations of New Age thought—even in the broadest analysis—represent an effort to put together a practical response to this distressing problem.

The Eastern view of evil has two central features. First and foremost, the concept of karma is everything. Born from an infinite number of prior births and deaths only to be reincarnated according to the cumulative good or evil you have done in your previous lives, the rewards and penalties for your deeds are in your own hands. In other words, by doing good you gradually progress to a higher level of being, but by doing evil you regress in caste or even in animal species. According to this system, the only hope of salvation from life's endless cycles of suffering, death and rebirth is an ultimate, final detachment from *everything*—including the physical universe itself.

The Eastern view of evil's second feature stresses that there is no answer to evil despite the belief that it is brutally real, central to, and forever inseparable from the character of everything that exists. Simply put, the universe is entirely evil and eternally incurable. Further, this malignant universe is regarded as an illusion even though it still afflicts people with real pain and despair in a life fraught with unanswerable questions.

Evil and Me

Twenty-six hundred years ago, the youthful innocence of Prince Siddhartha Gautama was shattered. His virgin observations of the death of his mother, the appalling sufferings of everyday life outside the walls of his cloistered existence, and the inevitability of death for all men devastated his naïve view of everything. Utterly dismayed, he declared, "Oh, worldly men! How fatal is your delusion! Inevitably your body will crumble to dust, yet carelessly, unheedingly, ye live on."[vii]

With this anguished cry, Siddhartha broke with his spoiled nobility and began a quest for the elimination of self, ultimately becoming the *Tathagata*—the one who was "gone." The "Buddha" was born—and so was the fundamental Eastern response to evil: the utter detachment from the material universe that both Hinduism and Buddhism view as irredeemable. As a result, the great pursuit of these ancient faiths became the "undifferentiated impersonal" — a permanent state of extinguishedness—the absorption of the individual self into the great deathless lake of Nirvana.

Evil and Us

A ninth century Hindu monk, Shankara, declared, "The relationship of God to the world is that of a dreamer to his dream. The dreamer alone is real; the world is unreal."[viii] This is the fundamental Eastern view of God and the world. Chasing this idea to its logical end, Shankara concluded life was like "the relationless relationship of the rope that is mistaken for the snake because of poor lighting. The rope appears as a snake no doubt, but actually there is no snake there, ever. Even when it appeared to be there, it was not there."[ix]

This, in turn, classifies the world as *maya*—a phenomenon of natural reality that is also a brief and fleeting mistake. A truly enlightened follower would hold that "the distinction between the self and the Universe is a false dichotomy. The distinction between consciousness and physical matter, between mind and body, is the result of an unenlightened perspective."[x] In other words, you would only believe the world is real out of pure ignorance.

This is enormously significant. If it is "god" who is dreaming and the true self along with everything else is merely his dream, then the repercussions concerning human rights, inalienable human dignity and genuine compassion are monumental. When god awakes, the illusion is over. If this is so, then, as R.C. Zaehner put it, "In practice it means that neither [Hinduism or Buddhism] in its classical formulation pays the slightest attention to what goes on in the world today."[xi]

The implications of the Eastern view of evil and human suffering are staggering, and the Eastern regard of the West's great efforts to relieve such evil and misery is one of narcissism and delusion.

Worlds in Collision

Despite its belief that life is but a dream, the Eastern view of evil is ironically realistic—so much so that its views on evil are largely in harmony with its Western monotheistic counterparts. Beyond this one point, however, similarities completely break down.

On the surface, this common ground with the West—the universal human experience of evil and suffering—has given rise to a host of Westernized-Eastern religious movements. These movements, which offer inner transformation, self-improvement and increased self-esteem include Transcendental Meditation, Positive Mental Attitude, various forms of yoga practices and, more recently, The Secret, A Course in Miracles, Conversations with God and the like. Major proponents of Westernized forms of Eastern thinking have included the Beatles, Oprah Winfrey, Helen Schucman, Barbara Marx Hubbard, Neal Donald Walsh, and Wayne Dyer.

The happy mysticism of these East-West religious hybrids, however, is eclipsed by the enormity of their fundamental religious differences with the West, having to do *not* with the reality of evil and suffering in the world, but what I can do about it for *me*.

The Eastern family of faith, as historically practiced, is a sea into which the average American would never fully immerse himself. Genuine Eastern religious philosophy is nearly untenable—even savage to the rational, self-oriented Western mind because its fatalistic denial of aspirations, hope and self, fly in the face of virtually all Western sensibilities. In fact, historical Eastern faiths adhere to fundamental beliefs deemed by the West as contrary to human rights, compassionate efforts on behalf of sufferers, earthly ambitions, self-improvement, conscious life after death, and endeavors to lessen the effects of evil. What, then, is the great dividing line between the historical Eastern faiths and the modern American hybrid religions?

In a word, *karma*.

Though it has always been a basic tenet of Buddhism, the idea of karma existed centuries before Siddhartha Gautama. Born out of a collision of logic and the problem of evil, the concept of karma teaches that we are all captive to an eternal cycle of reincarnation based on the ethical and moral qualities of our own actions. In other words, the good or evil we suffer in our present life is the cause-and-effect result of the actions of our past lives— of which we are solely responsible. According to the Mahabharata, "Since man lives under the control of karma, he must always be alert to ways of maintaining his equilibrium and avoiding evil consequences."[xii] In other words, our present station in life, whether poor or rich, coddled or afflicted, is our karmically determined, inescapable fate in our most recent incarnation of life. This explains the many disparities and injustices in the world, as well as the level of evil and suffering people must endure according to their karma.

Burmese Buddhist monk and meditation master Mahasi Sayadaw put it like this:

"According to Buddhism, this inequality is due not only to heredity, environment, 'nature and nurture,' but also to karma. In other words, it is the result of our own past actions and our own present doings. We ourselves are responsible for our own happiness and misery. We create our own Heaven. We create our own Hell. We are the architects of our own fate."[xiii]

When a young seeker asked the Buddha about the injustices of human experience, he answered, "All living beings have actions as their own, their inheritance, their congenital cause, their kinsman, their refuge. It is karma that differentiates beings into low and high states."[xiv]

What is the logical outcome? Karma, as practiced by the Eastern family of faiths, has produced few or no humanitarian, compassionate, or human rights efforts—mainly because the evil that people suffer is the assured result of their own past actions. Thus, it is the betterment of my own self that should be my greatest concern, while all others are doomed to embrace their own karma. Mahasi Sayadaw enthusiastically agreed:

> "A Buddhist who is fully convinced of the law of karma does not pray to another to be saved, but confidently relies on him[self] for his own emancipation. Instead of making any self-surrender, or calling on any supernatural agency, he relies on his own will power, and works incessantly for the well-being and happiness of all. This belief in karma validates his effort and kindles his enthusiasm, because it teaches individual responsibility. To the ordinary Buddhist, karma

serves as a deterrent, while to an intellectual, it serves as an incentive to do good. He or she becomes kind, tolerant, and considerate. This law of karma explains the problem of suffering, the mastery of so-called fate and predestination of other religions and about all the inequality of mankind."[xv]

Despite Buddhism's reputation for tolerance, kindness and consideration for others, the idea of karma has to do solely with *my* own efforts on *my* own behalf. Although Sayadaw suggests that karma promotes "working incessantly for the well-being of others," his picture of the Buddhist response to human suffering is inherently *self*—not *others*—oriented.

Boston College philosophy professor Dr. Peter Kreeft put it like this:

"[For] Spiritual athletes who practice [various forms of] Yoga or the Buddhist Noble Eight-Fold Path, pain is abolished by abolishing its root: desire. When there are no desires left, there are no frustrations left. Hindu or Buddhist Yoga can succeed by killing off the desires. The true Buddhist does overcome all pain, but also all pleasure; all fear, but also all hope; all hate, but also all love; all misery, but also all joy. This is a remarkable achievement, but is it worth the price of half our human nature? It looks like spiritual euthanasia: killing the patient to cure the disease."[xvi]

The ultimate goal of karma is still Nirvana—the extinguishing of the self—the undifferentiated impersonal where there is no I, me, us, they, them or we. It is the place where earthly hope and aspiration are rendered irrelevant. And it is here where the Eastern family of faiths collides head-on with the West—the East being clearly world-denying, the West openly world-affirming.

Further, although Buddhist and Hindu cultures have historically demonstrated tremendous aptitude in mathematics, technology and medicine, nearly all expressions of humanitarianism have been sorely missing except as a byproduct of Western intervention. The idea of hospitals was not a development of Eastern religious thinking, nor were benevolent organizations, chaplaincies, disaster relief agencies, or almost any other means designed to alleviate the acknowledged impact of evil. Economic disparities between East and West can be cited, but the global pattern of disaster relief efforts has proven to be an act of moral will for participating nations, not funding. But for Buddhism, Hinduism and their countless offshoots, "there is no remedy for evil in or for this world; there is only renunciation of this world."[xvii]

Such is the legacy of karma: evil is intensely real, and one must work to counter it in his or her own life in order to evolve to a higher circle of being. As for the misery of others, "Why should I help? It is their karma. What can I do about it? What can *anyone* do about it? What *should* anyone do about it—they brought it upon themselves. It is their fault, not mine." With karma, life is, in the end, *every man for himself.*

But there are other, more unsettling questions posed by the idea of karma: what about the prosperous villain, the cruel and narcissistic billionaire or the immoral, sadistic rock star? What does karma have to say for the sexually abused baby, the battered wife, or the tortured martyr? Are they truly reaping the justice of their karma? What about the disproportionate prosperity of Westerners over the Central, Southern, and Southeast Asians who are dedicated adherents to Hinduism and Buddhism—those who are religiously (and thus culturally) consigned to endure mind-bending poverty and disease? Are Westerners so much more virtuous than they?[2]

A Rather Eastern Western Idea

Stoicism, possibly the most Eastern and most prevalent of the Western philosophies, suggests that people use good thinking to

[2] Westerners who hold to a West-East hybrid of Eastern religion yet who are determined to act benevolently on an individual or corporate basis (essentially others-centered) are, ironically, acting in opposition to historical Eastern thought and much more in accord with historical Christianity.

lessen suffering, enabling a separation from the agony of a bad situation. In a sense, Western Stoicism has, from its beginnings, unintentionally echoed some of the philosophical underpinnings of Eastern religion, bridging the chasm between Eastern and modern Western ideology. Undiluted Stoicism, however, is entirely unfriendly to the soft, self-absorbed Western mind. Like its Eastern equivalents, true Stoic detachment demands an emotional aloofness from evil and suffering that most Westerners would rather confront head-on.

The emotional indifference of Stoicism demands a broader perspective of life, a "standing back" in order to observe the whole landscape of life. "Things are not as bad as they appear," a good Stoic would say, and, "this, too, shall pass."

In the words of Seneca, "Happy is the man who can endure the highest and lowest fortune. He who endured such vicissitudes with equanimity has deprived misfortune of its power."[xviii] Marcus Aurelius declared, "If you are distressed by anything external, the pain is not due to the thing itself but to your estimate of it; and this you have the power to revoke at any moment."[xix] An internet blogger noted, "Being able to cope with the best of times and the worst of times requires skill and knowledge…. To cope with these eventualities, we need to know that they will come, both the good and the bad, and that we will survive them and return to some sort of normal state of life." He concluded, "Bad always passes…for everyone, so long as they live through it. Exceptionally good times don't last forever.... Just knowing that much makes us prepared to [better] face the ups and downs of life."[xx] Statements like these bring to light the Stoic roots of the resilient, naturalistic optimism of the prosperous West.

But even though Stoicism's pseudo-Eastern ideas have blended with modern Western thought, it hardly works in the Eastern mind. Buddhism and Hinduism have an enormously broad perspective of evil and suffering, spanning lifetimes and uncounted generations, with the goal of ultimate detachment from every earthly thing. But their universal perspective, regardless of the optimism of Eastern advocates like Sayadaw, is intensely fatalistic. Looking on "the bright side of life" in the midst of a brutally realistic view of evil and suffering is unfathomable to the Easterner.

Stoicism's notions of emotional divorce from evil and suffering soars, however, in the prosperous, self-absorbed West, which rarely encounters pain and loss on the level of its Eastern counterparts. Mark Twain once observed, "Nothing that grieves us can be called little, for by the eternal laws of proportion a child's loss of a doll and a king's loss of a crown are events of the same size."[xxi] In other words, "a good perspective and a sense of proportion" is all we need to ease the pain of suffering—at least in the dreams of the thriving, sheltered, modern West.

> "If there is no self, whose arthritis is this?"
> —Sayings of the Jewish Buddha

THE SECULAR VIEW OF EVIL

"[Man is] united with his fellow-men by the strongest of all ties, the tie of a common doom…"

—Bertrand Russell

"Between 1800 and 1900 the doctrine of Pie in the Sky gave place, in a majority of Western minds, to the doctrine of Pie on Earth."

—Aldous Huxley

Secularism is a subject rarely cited outside sociological lectures and civil libertarian think tanks—but Secularism is a big word that embodies an enormous and rapidly expanding family of faith.

Common secularism is made up of an assortment of humanism, atheism, naturalism, relativism, rationalism, Darwinism and scientism—whose view of reality can be summed up in the mantra, "chance plus matter plus time." Secularism believes that science and rationalism has made the idea of God obsolete, along with all the absolute values associated with Him. It is far from a united family of faith, and many of its views about suffering, evil, truth and compassion are erratic and conflicted. Secularism's umbrella belief, however, unifies its many divisions: God must bow to science. But this is by no means a recent idea.

The philosophy of Epicurus (341-270 BC) is probably the deepest root of today's secularist view of evil. Epicurus, who was both an Atomist and Hedonist, taught that evil was devoid of supernatural origin and influence, reducing it to the mere absence of pleasure. He concluded, "All objects and events—including human lives—are nothing more than physical interactions among minute indestructible particles." In other words, everything occurs entirely by chance.

This was the basis of Epicurus' ideas about ethics and evil and the foundation of Epicureanism. In a letter to one of his contemporaries, Menoeceus, he wrote:

> "While therefore all pleasure because it is naturally akin to us is good, not all pleasure is worthy of choice, just as all pain is an evil and yet not all pain is to be shunned. It is, however, by measuring one against another, and by looking at the conveniences and inconveniences, that all these matters must be judged...For the end of all our actions is to be free from pain and fear, and, when once we have attained all this, the tempest of the soul is laid; seeing that the living creature has no need to go in

search of something that is lacking, nor to look for anything else by which the good of the soul and of the body will be fulfilled. When we are pained because of the absence of pleasure, then, and then only, do we feel the need of pleasure. Wherefore we call pleasure the alpha and omega of a blessed life. Pleasure is our first and kindred good. It is the starting-point of every choice and of every aversion, and to it we come back, inasmuch as we make feeling the rule by which to judge of every good thing."[xxii]

Simply put, to the Epicurean, evil was the absence of pleasure or the presence of pain, but such evil was not necessarily all bad or something to be avoided since its relative intensity enhanced its contrasting pleasures.

Two millennia later, Scottish philosopher and skeptic Dr. David Hume reasoned that since an omniscient God must be aware of evil, an omnipotent God could prevent evil, and a benevolent God would not tolerate evil, it should follow that there is no evil.[xxiii] It must also follow that there is no God, for evil cannot exist apart from a sovereign God who is in every way both absolute and absolutely good. But if God exists, whether compassionate or not, then evil *as evil* must also exist, because a sovereign God unmoved by man's subjective judgments would stand as the absolute measure of all things.

Hume's assertions, like those of so many other critics of God and evil, were in fact a matter of personal conviction. In his strong distaste for belief in something that he could not scientifically quantify, he unintentionally contradicted his own philosophy: he *presumed*. Presumption is not scientific, it is a *belief*—which, for Hume, seems to have erupted out of his personal contempt for the idea of a God who would not live up to his own expectations.

Like Hume, modern critics of faith in God—especially the Judeo-Christian view—suggest that it is impossible to imagine, much less decipher how a loving God could allow evil and do little or nothing to hinder it.[xxiv] And the logic here is peculiar: *Evil cannot exist as evil because God allows it, yet God cannot exist because He allows evil.*

Such logic leaves us with our feet firmly planted in mid-air. This sort of presumption allows anyone to define evil anyway they want (including no definition at all) when God is forced out of the picture. Evil can once again be downgraded to the mere natural impact of some valueless thing that has meddled in our pleasure or caused our pain. But even *that,* according to secular philosophers and empiricists, could be considered a form of evil, because it was judged as wrong and resisted according to our stubborn sense of fairness. This is a troubling paradox to secularists, because the cast-off values of an abandoned God have a curious habit of turning up during the next crisis.

It's Only Natural

Not many years after Hume, Charles Darwin shook the world with his book, "On the Origin of Species", igniting a philosophical firestorm that still rages in the West. Darwin's theories greased the cogs of secular thought, bringing about an ever-increasing number of *isms*, including the ancient philosophy of scientific *naturalism*.

Naturalism, which was practiced before the time of Socrates, argues that all human suffering is the result of random forces of nature and is therefore entirely without purpose or reason. Such a bleak point of view is actually quite reasonable in the realm of Darwinism, which itself has evolved into the sacred path of the truly enlightened. As a result, many of today's philosophical movements are heavily naturalistic, and the hallways of our modern schools and universities resonate with its heady but hollow echo.

But people do not usually see life that way—not because they do not want to, but because they cannot seem to view anything, especially suffering, as empty of all meaning. People— even the ones who hotly oppose the existence of God and the supernatural—seem driven to *assign* meaning to just about everything. In other words, as a species we do not merely *perceive* the cosmos around us, but we are compelled to explore and calculate its qualities. But far beyond that, we are also able to *understand* and *appreciate* its processes. Because we possess these transcendent capacities, the evidence suggests that we are inherently bound to consider our place in the midst of everything that is.

Astronomer and cosmologist Carl Sagan said of humanity, "We are [all] star-stuff."[xxv] He encapsulated in this tiny phrase the sweeping assertion that all life on earth (or in the universe, for that matter) is "the assured result of the accidental accumulation and arrangement of heavier elements birthed by supernovae during one of the more recent evolutionary epochs of the cosmos. Hence, the basic scientific appraisal of humanity suggests that animate matter, born of random natural processes, spontaneously developed a capacity for self-awareness on its brief march towards inevitable extinction," or something like that. Simply put, life just *is*, and it exists without the possibility of ever possessing any meaning.

According to Sagan, humanity is a lucky cosmological hiccup, and the best anyone can do is enjoy the ride before all life dissolves into a futile, forgetful infinity. Even so, he still seemed compelled to assign to it a simple but crucial purpose when he wrote, "Our loyalties are to the species and the planet. We speak for Earth. Our obligation to survive is owed not just to ourselves but also to that Cosmos, ancient and vast, from which we spring."[xxvi]

Dr. Sagan remained steadfast in his conviction of a meaningless cosmos. Of their final moments together, his longtime companion, Ann Druyan wrote: "Contrary to the fantasies of the fundamentalists, there was no deathbed conversion, no last-minute refuge taken in a comforting vision of a heaven or an afterlife. For

Carl, what mattered most was what was true, not merely what would make us feel better. Even at this moment when anyone would be forgiven for turning away from the reality of our situation, Carl was unflinching. As we looked deeply into each other's eyes, it was with a shared conviction that our wondrous life together was ending forever."[xxvii] Ironically, in such a cosmos not even human tragedy can be considered reasonable to a species that is resigned to its own doom—such is a place where evil would be ridiculous.

Other secular thinkers and scientists set out on a different quest for the Holy Grail of meaning, delving deep into the human genetic code. There, within the vast, winding strands of human DNA, they hope to identify a mysterious gene that will give a biochemical explanation for our dogged demand for significance, and perhaps even our sense of God. But such a discovery, even if it were scientifically confirmed, would prove little. As geneticist and biochemist Dr. A.E. Wilder-Smith observed:

> "Where our forefathers based their thought processes on the premise that life and the universe were meaningful, thought processes today are governed by exactly the opposite premise. Sartre, Camus and other modern thinkers have obtained the highest praise from today's intelligentsia for elegantly and cleverly conveying the premise that life, man, and the universe are meaningless. It

naturally follows, therefore, that suffering is meaningless, too. According to this view, the mixtures of amino acids that are supposed to have given spontaneous birth to life showed no meaning or motivation behind them; no volition guided these and other building blocks into the codes of meaning that make up DNA as we know it today. The first nucleic acids and proteins allegedly arose spontaneously from meaninglessness. This boils down to saying that if there is any meaning in life or its origin at all, that meaning must be based on sheer meaningless. The same applies to life's destiny—it must be meaningless, too."[xxviii]

Biologist and radical atheist Richard Dawkins wrote, "If there is mercy in nature, it is accidental. Nature is neither kind nor cruel but indifferent."[xxix] But how do we know that is true? Dawkins' declaration seems quite absolute in a universe that he insists has no absolutes. As was the case with Hume, would not such a pronouncement be more presumption than scientific? A similar statement in any other context would likely be condemned as naïvely dogmatic, and in this case, scientistic pigheadedness. Like Dawkins and Hume, as the secularist attempts to assign meaning or meaninglessness to life, man, the universe and suffering, he will ultimately, if not unwittingly, yield to a relentless, loathsome demon: *faith*.

Here is the problem: in secularism, suffering and evil are recognized as real because they are felt through experiences, but neither must ever be called *true*. Yet it would be foolish to declare either one as meaningless and walk away, for evil will not be walked away from. Like a naughty child, it taunts the tormented mind to search harder and harder for an answer to its overwhelming pain and elusive meaning, luring it down a path that will end in anguished despair or unreasonable faith. To the secularist, neither is acceptable, and one is intolerable.

It seems that the quest for a world dominated by pure reason has failed miserably trying to provide a new evolution of human meaning. No grail brimming with purpose has been handed humanity, for though the quest continues, the cup will never be found—not because it is lost, but because it never existed. Reason seems to have robbed people of reasons.

"It all Depends..."

Ideas have consequences. The idea that evil does not exist in a naturalistic world has huge and dangerous consequences. In fact, rather than freeing mankind from the burden of evil *as evil*, it makes him a slave to it.

Alexander Solzhenitsyn understood it first-hand:

"Such a tilt of freedom in the direction of evil has come about gradually but it was evidently born primarily out of a humanistic and benevolent concept according to which there is no evil inherent to human nature; the world belongs to mankind and all the defects of life are caused by wrong social systems which must be corrected. Strangely enough, though the best social conditions have been achieved in the West, there still is criminality and there even is considerably more of it than in the pauper and lawless Soviet society. We turned our backs upon the Spirit and embraced all that is material with excessive and unwarranted zeal. This new way of thinking, which had imposed on us its guidance, did not admit the existence of intrinsic evil in man nor did it see any higher task than the attainment of happiness on earth. It based modern Western civilization on the dangerous trend to worship man and his material needs. Everything beyond physical well-being and accumulation of material goods, all other human requirements and characteristics of a subtler and higher nature, were left outside the area of attention of state and social systems, as if human life did not have any superior sense. That provided access for evil, of which in our days there is a free and constant flow. Mere freedom does not in the least solve all the problems of human life and it even adds a number of new ones."[xxx]

A few years ago, a loose association of secularists and militant atheists set out on a campaign of disinformation, seeking to fortify their own ideology. Particularly persuasive on university campuses and the talk-show circuit, these intellectuals accused religion (chiefly Christianity) of being the well and trough of humanity's most horrendous atrocities. During a lecture at Harvard University author and activist Gore Vidal, an avid supporter of this strategy, declared: "The great unmentionable evil at the center of our culture is monotheism."[xxxi] Many other influential secularists have made similar and very public allegations. History, on the other hand, paints a radically different picture.

In the Twentieth Century alone, secularist ideologues led Utopian regimes in unleashing upon humanity the most unspeakable carnage of any age in recorded history. Even though monotheism has been sweepingly indicted as the source of virtually all the social evils of the last two thousand years, they have yet to offer any evidence aside from the usual charges levied at the Crusades and the Inquisitions—both of which were trivial compared with the lethal impact of secularism on the modern world.[3]

On the other hand, the mountain of historical data concerning those responsible for the death, suffering and torture of

---

[3] The number of deaths attributed to the Crusades, both Moslem and Christian, soldier and civil (including disease-related fatalities) is liberally estimated to be around 200,000; the estimated number of deaths attributed to the Inquisitions is loosely estimated around 11,000.

hundreds of millions of people in the last century falls squarely on a different set of shoulders. To be sure, various sects of the monotheistic Islamic religion have proven themselves notorious in their coercive evangelistic and domination efforts, accounting for the death and suffering of several million—most recently during the interval of 1915 to 1923 when the Muslim Young Turks tried to annihilate the Christian Armenians.[4] On the other hand, the slaughter of the Bosnian Moslems during the 1990's and the violent sectarian conflicts of Northern Ireland were carried out by traditionally Christian *political* factions, which in no way mirrored Biblical Christian theology.

According to the Encyclopedia of Genocide,

"In total, during the first eighty-eight years of [the twentieth] century, almost 170 million men, women, and children were shot, beaten, tortured, knifed, burned, starved, frozen, crushed, or worked to death; buried alive, drowned, hanged, bombed, or killed in any other of the myriad other ways governments have inflicted deaths on unarmed, helpless citizens and foreigners. Depending on whether one used high or more conservative estimates, the dead could conceivably be more than

---

[4] Actual deaths attributed to Islamic expansionism over the past fourteen centuries have been recently estimated to be around 270,000,000, or an average of 192,800 people killed every year since its founding.

360 million people. It is as though our species has been devastated by a modern Black Plague."[xxxii]

A simple survey of the data reveals that the appalling numbers of dead, maimed and dispossessed were victims of secularist regimes working to transform the world according to their Utopianist ideologies:

Joseph Stalin	More than 42,000,000 (1929-53)
Mao Tse-tung	More than 37,000,000 (1923-76)
Adolf Hitler	More than 20,000,000 (1933-45)
Vladimir Lenin	More than 4,000,000 (1917-1924)
Hideki Tojo	Nearly 4,000,000 (1937-1944)
Pol Pot	More than 2,000,000 (1975-79)

These estimates are considered extremely conservative—actual figures are believed to be significantly higher. And this short list does not include the carnage perpetrated by North Korea's Kim Il Sung and the upheavals in the Congo, Cuba, Nicaragua, Peru, Southeast Asia, and the like.[xxxiii] In fact, as a result of secularist attempts to impose on the world some form of utopian ideology, it is estimated that more people were slaughtered in the twentieth century than *lived* in any other previous century.

Aside from Islamist atrocities, however, the monotheistic religions of Christianity and Judaism played a relatively unappreciable (though nonetheless dastardly) role in the bloodshed of the last century. This comparatively meager number of cruel and immoral acts, however, in no way justifies the oppression or death of a single innocent soul in the name of Christ. Moreover, even a single incident of deadly Christian injustice against another (of which there were unquestionably many hundreds of thousands since Pentecost) is utterly contradictory to the nature of Christ and, according to the Scriptures, reprehensible and even damnable.

Secularism, on the other hand, could never honestly offer such a confession of its own evils because it fundamentally rejects evil as a factor in the moral measure of things. Whatever meaning might lie behind any action, even genocide, a moral judgment of such would merely be relative and subject to the majority vote or to those with the loudest voice.

In a system of belief that seeks to cut itself off from the objective roots of moral and ethical boundaries, could anyone truly applaud any act as virtuous, or revile it as monstrous?

The only reasonable answer would be, "It all depends…"

Stubborn Morality

Every interpretation of right and wrong is a moral one, regardless of one's belief system. The question is which belief system should we embrace to establish our morality? According to secularism, mankind is obligated to reject any fixed basis for morality, lest he affirm "irrational" religion and the possibility of a real, sovereign God. In an empty universe, both pleasure and suffering must be viewed as naturally occurring physical responses with no reasonable purpose. Declaring anything *good* or *evil* would be naïve, except as a subjective response to pleasure or unpleasantness. As fleeting particles in a great, uncaring cosmos, who among us could truly dictate the moral value of anything?

Only a person of questionable sanity would argue that pain or displeasure doesn't hurt. But any attempt by a secularist to interpret the wrongness or rightness of *anything* affirms a belief system that contradicts their belief in a random universe. Yet such belief is among the most basic ingredients of human nature, namely the inevitable (to the secularist, awkward) human habit of automatically interpreting the moral value of any thing or event.

According to secularism, everything that exists ultimately lacks meaning, yet a tension simmers behind this mode of thinking, because even its staunchest adherents regularly determine value and explore meaning as life happens to them and around them. Good and evil will inevitably occur in everyday life, yet both transcend reason. In fact, they stubbornly defy rational containment—and suffering, in particular, insists it be given meaning.

Secular Morality

"People like me only have a duty to ourselves; we have no duty to other people…I am responsible only to the reality that I know, and absolutely not responsible to anything else." —Mao Tse-tung

Secularism is a volatile philosophy—it is an ever-shifting Rubik's Cube of beliefs, scientific assumptions and theological presumptions. For instance, adherents to the Documentary Hypothesis and Higher Criticism (the modern rationalist method of interpreting the Bible) insist that miracles do not happen and God does not speak to people, not because they can prove these assertions, but because they are simply not rational. Many scholars and theologians hold this position as fact, but it proceeds from a platform of presumption. In other words, "God must be a certain way because I cannot imagine Him being a different way."

Atheist and secularist Richard Dawkins, author of *The God Delusion*, scorns the idea of God, blaming belief in Him for the bulk of the world's social and moral ills: "The God of the Old Testament is arguably the most unpleasant character in all fiction: jealous and proud of it; a petty, unjust, unforgiving control-freak; a vindictive, bloodthirsty ethnic cleaner; a misogynistic, homophobic, racist, infanticidal, genocidal, filicidal, pestilentialm, megalomaniacal, sadomasochistic, capriciously malevolent bully."[xxxiv]

Though the sheer verbal force of Dawkins' scathing diatribe conveys a certain academic authority, when examined, his "theology" is derived from the written moral values of the same God he is attacking, thus validating Yahweh as his authoritative source of moral evaluation. Further, though the theology of Richard Dawkins is provocative, it gives the impression of a fanatical deophobia—especially of the God of the Bible. But his relentless effort to incite a public and visceral hatred of God raises an interesting question: why attack this particular God more than the others?

Like the Eastern and New Age smorgasbord of philosophies, secularism is forced to remain a fluid and somewhat ambiguous belief system in order to avoid serious self-contradiction. Gazing across the landscape of its claims, it becomes increasingly clear that secularism's doctrine is neither reasonable nor sound, employing the same absolutes that it must also utterly deny.

To declare something true, one *must* provide the objective authority to say so, yet such an idea is hostile to the general tenets of secularism. Even so, dedicated secularists will often label as evil anyone who holds fast to absolutes—which is, of course, a moral judgment of the same order. In this light, secular doctrine is revealed as little more than a failed, contaminated relativism. But this also is nothing new.

Relativism has been around a long time. According to the Encyclopedia of Religion, relativism urges "the suspension of judgment about right and wrong."[xxxv] More than three thousand years ago an unidentified author recorded the cause of the social calamity afflicting ancient Israel during the time of the Judges, writing, "In those days there was no king in Israel; every man did that which was right in his own eyes." Accordingly, a people guided by their own relativistic whims are likely to fare no better than the Israelites—who in those days had completely lost their way.

World history reminds us that the strong will ultimately concoct ways to impose their idea of a greater good with moral impunity. This is an oft-repeated story line to which, in just the last century, hundreds of millions of the dead and despairing now stand as the spectral witnesses to its cataclysmic whims.

Evil on the Couch

"Psychological laws that govern human well-being [will eventually provide] an enduring basis for objective morality."[xxxvi]

—Sam Harris, Atheist

"A science which does not bring us nearer to God is worthless."[xxxvii]

—Simone Weil

Secularism is convinced that virtually all our questions about life and meaning—including evil and suffering—will be answered by science. Driven by this idea, human behavioral scientists have rigorously sought to explain "negative" human behavior. This focus rests solidly on a non-faith platform, because, as with most other sciences, religion is considered superstitious and therefore incompatible with behavioral studies.

In his introductory lecture to a class of young psychology students, a bespectacled, goateed Orange Coast College professor declared that all human behavior was void of spiritual meaning and influence, especially "negative behaviors" that ignorant people assigned to satanic origin. He confidently asserted, "'The devil made me do it' is the great excuse for all the bad things people do—but we all *know* there is no devil…"

We all know there is no devil?

We do?

To the contrary, the vast majority of the world's population professes some sort of belief in the existence of a corrupt, relentlessly evil being that mercilessly afflicts people everywhere. In fact, this belief is held by as many as 2.2 billion Christians, 1.5 billion Muslims, 900 million Hindus, 376 million Buddhists, and more than a half a billion other followers of lesser religious orders and cults.[xxxviii] This amounts to more than five-sixths of the world's inhabitants. Such statistics do not necessarily make a thing true, but neither can such a widespread idea be so handily dismissed.

Behavioral science has historically argued that belief in the supernatural is best set aside when confronting issues of human behavior. Despite this rational approach, the overwhelmingly widespread belief in a devil is compelling and suggests otherwise. The ash-heaps of humanity's progress loom as appalling witnesses to the schemes of unseen malevolent forces hard at work. But what if science is right and the devil is nothing more than primitive myth? What, then, would be the *real* devil in a world gone so obviously wrong?

During a 1972 Youth for Christ conference a popular Christian minister spoke for several sessions on the doctrine of sin. Addressing thousands of High School youth, he repeatedly replaced the word "sin" with the phrase "negative behavior" in the hope of making an unpopular subject more relevant to the younger generation. From a scientific viewpoint, this would be a fitting description, provided you could determine the moral meaning of "negative." But applying such an expression to an essential Christian doctrine secularized a spiritual axiom. In other words, the Christian speaker, wittingly or unwittingly, undermined the sinfulness of sin and weakened the significance of spiritual evil and mankind's moral culpability. Therapy had just supplanted theology—and the teenagers never knew the better.

Humanity is marked by its unyielding resolve to master its own environment and destiny. Yet no other age of history has witnessed mankind array himself in robes of sacred self-importance as he has in this modern world. He has flaunted his sense of evolved superiority by reducing his treacherous human nature to a set of presumptions based on observation and behavioral analysis. To his credit, this has resulted in some remarkable studies in conditioned response, traumatic stress, forms of psychoanalysis and the like, but none of it has adequately accounted for the basest nature of man. Sin and evil resist a scientific reckoning. The challenge of evil still lurks just beyond the reach of the most enlightened efforts to contain, mediate or rehabilitate it.

Attorney Clarence Darrow wrote, "Science and evolution teach us that man is an animal, a little higher than the other orders of animals; that he is governed by the same natural laws that govern the rest of the universe." Darrow championed the idea of interpreting a person's actions, whether right or wrong, solely in the light of their childhood experiences finding expression in adult life. "Therefore," he reasoned, "how could any individual be responsible for his or her actions if they were predetermined?"[xxxix]

Os Guinness, on the other hand, observed, "Many people today believe—or at least act as if they believe—that all the answers they need in life come from science. But as brilliant and helpful as the natural sciences are, they are not competent to speak of evil, for evil cannot be seen, touched, weighed, or measured with any of the senses."[xl]

"Negative behavior" is a fitting description of a harmful act to self or to others, but it does not account for the intense feelings of guilt and shame that accompany the "negative" deed. Nor has behavioral analysis offered an adequate explanation for man's universal gravitation toward hurtful conduct. Science suggests that negative tendencies might be an echo—a malignant relic of mankind's slow evolutionary climb out of a savage past. But man is also proud, holding fast to his rightness and supremacy in the glare of his own moral defects. He must have the one but cannot rid himself of the other. His "negative behavior" appears to draw its nourishment from deep and rotten roots.

In the noir movie *Chinatown,* villain Noah Cross chided the hapless anti-hero, J.J. Gittes: "I don't blame myself. You see, Mr. Gittes, most people never have to face the fact that at the right time and the right place, they're capable of *anything* [emphasis in the script]." This chilling line is wickedly cynical, but history reminds us that it is also painfully true.

Evil insists on having its way, and man has proven himself powerless to prevent or adequately reduce its deep-seeded malevolence on any scientific level. In fact, in the course of behavioral science's quest to cure negative human behavior, our societal and behavioral state of affairs has conspicuously deteriorated. And the reason may be more self-evident than science cares to admit.

Aldous Huxley seemed to agree when he wrote, "Out of the illimitable blackness of the world the light of his customary thinking scoops, as it were, a little illuminated cave—a tunnel of brightness, in which, from the brink of consciousness to its death, he lives, moves, and has his being…We ignore the outer darkness; or if we cannot ignore it, if it presses too insistently upon us, we disapprove of being afraid."[xli]

When we speak of evil, even with the rancor of my Orange Coast College psychology professor, there must still be an attributing source. For the professor it could never be the devil, for in order to advance as a species, rational, thinking people must come to the belief that evil, as a distinct force, cannot really exist. "It is negative behavior which must be accounted for," he would contend, "and because evil is not tangible or measurable, and since the supernatural is absurd, evil and the devil are primitive superstitions and thus forbidden factors in the equation."

C.S. Lewis offered a counterproposal in his speculative book, *The Screwtape Letters*. Advising his underling minion about how he could ruin the spiritual life of his human "patient," the fictitious demon, Uncle Screwtape, wrote,

> "We are really faced with a cruel dilemma. When the humans disbelieve in our existence we lose all the pleasing results of direct terrorism and we make no magicians. On the other hand, when they believe in us, we cannot make them materialists and skeptics. At least, not yet. I have great hopes that we shall learn in due time how to emotionalize and mythologize their science to such an extent that what is, in effect, belief in us, (though not under that name) will creep in while the human mind remains closed to belief in the Enemy [God]. The 'Life Force,' the worship of sex, and some aspects of Psychoanalysis may here prove useful. If once we can produce our perfect work—the Materialist Magician, the man, not using, but veritably

worshipping, what he vaguely calls 'Forces' while denying the existence of 'spirits'—then the end of the war will be in sight. Deep inside we know that the facts of the matter are not the end of the matter...I do not think you will have much difficulty in keeping the patient in the dark. The fact that 'devils' are predominantly comic figures in the modern imagination will help you. If any faint suspicion of your existence begins to arise in his mind, suggest to him a picture of something in red tights, and persuade him that since he cannot believe in that (it is an old textbook method of confusing them) he therefore cannot believe in you."[xlii]

"It was through pride that the devil became the devil,"[xliii] Lewis once noted. Man seems to have followed not too far behind.

Reluctant Cousins

Friedrich Nietzsche was deeply moved by the spectacular vistas of Alpine valleys—placid emerald chasms sculpted by centuries of massive, grinding glaciers. Inspired by the idea that violent natural forces could create splendor, he famously proclaimed, "What does not kill me makes me stronger."[xliv]

Such a remarkable observation by a militant atheist is, ironically, Biblical in its portrayal of the effect of natural forces on people, lacking only the purposefulness of divine sovereignty. This romantic notion became the basis for Nietzsche's expansion on the Darwinian concept of the evolutionary ascension of man into super-man, densely depicted in his book, *Also Spake Zarathustra*. In it he concluded that evil and suffering were real, and that man had the supreme obligation to defy them both, battling ever onward toward his divine destiny.

This ideal is, however, not *exclusively* humanistic. The Judeo-Christian view of evil is nearly identical, not in its purpose, but in its *purposefulness*. For both the secularist and Western families of faith, evil is a thing to be actively combated and countered—it is to be openly resisted, because according to both belief systems it obstructs and corrupts aspirations of happiness, dominance and creativity. Though no two ideologies could be more radically disconnected, they both share the conviction that evil must be opposed for the greater good of one and all.

But the similarities end there. The Judeo-Christian concept of evil holds to an objective definition of evil and the existence of an objective *Definer*. Secularism, on the other hand, votes on the meaning of its own perceived evils and then opposes them without the benefit of a standard candle of moral measurement in a universe that, according to their faith, is both voiceless and indifferent.

Both families of faith possess this limited but important commonality; the former does so in faith, the latter in idealistic dishonesty.

> "THE GOOD and THE BAD had been popular once, but that was when rumors of GOD were rife. THE GOOD was GOD's holy character and had to be obeyed. THE BAD was disobedience or revolt against THE GOOD. But THE GOOD and THE BAD departed with REASON and GOD. And now there was no longer TRAGEDY—only MISERY."[xlv]
>
> —The Western Book of the Dead

THE WESTERN VIEW OF EVIL

"All things work for the good of those who love God and are called according to His purpose."

—The Apostle Paul, Romans 8:28

"Every happening, great and small, is a parable whereby God speaks to us, and the art of life is to get the message."

—Malcolm Muggeridge

"God can do anything!" On the surface, it makes perfect sense: after all, He *is* God. When you really consider the possibilities, this simple phrase can be rather terrifying. But according to the Western, or Judeo-Christian[5] view of everything, there are (happily) some things God just cannot do. According to the Bible God cannot lie, die, sin, break any of His promises or do things

---

[5] Since Islam is essentially a hybrid of Hebraic and regional Semitic pagan ideologies, its view of evil and suffering closely mirror the typical Western view; thus its merits will not be discussed here at any length.

that would ever violate His nature. No matter what, He cannot do evil.

God is *holy*—utterly, infinitely, and eternally separate from unholiness—which makes Him incapable of being or doing evil. This is not to say that God is incapable of preventing evil or even using it for His own purposes or glorification: He is, and He does.

The Eastern concept of evil teaches that the world is and always has been incurably evil, and that the only good that can come of it is the attainment of that impersonal nothingness called Nirvana.

The secular view suggests that because life is a lucky combination of random matter and forces, evil as a concept is a product of our superstitious ignorance. To the secularist this concept becomes a nagging obstacle to pure reason and the evolution of the species.

The Judeo-Christian concept of evil, in contrast, declares that though the world is awash in evil and suffering, it did not begin that way. Even more, the Bible teaches that God is so angry about evil that He personally paid the price to ensure its abolition.

More than a Message

Not long after the Day of Pentecost—a Jewish feast held in Jerusalem that became the inception day of the church—the Gospel began to spread rapidly through Asia Minor and North Africa. Its ideas of grace, forgiveness, resurrection and salvation enthralled the vast assortment of pagan peoples of the Greco-Roman world. It was astonishing, in fact, that the simple message of a persecuted Jewish sect founded by a crucified peasant-Rabbi would so quickly captivate the spiritual sensibilities of a largely Greek-thinking, polytheistic population ruled by a string of Imperial despots. Mark Galli, editor of *Christianity Today*, observed,

> "The early church didn't have a Graham, a Finney, or a Moody. It didn't have Promise Keepers, a Great Awakening, or User-Friendly churches. Furthermore, it had no concise spiritual laws to share, no explosive method for talking to the unconverted. What it had seems quite paltry: it had unspectacular people with a hodgepodge of methods, so hodgepodge that they can hardly be called methods, and rarely a gathering of more than a handful of people. The paltry seems to have been enough, however, to make an emperor or two stop and take notice…[It is] a hodgepodge of [what]…normal, and to us, nameless Christians did to bring the Name of Jesus Christ to the attention of pagans; not a phenomenon that filled stadiums, just enough to begin converting the whole known world…"

Judeo-Christianity flourished in the Eastern thought

process, even while it flowed contrary to Eastern religious philosophy. The Roman Empire and its pagan tributaries, however, lacked the Hindu-Buddhist fatalism and resignation to evil and suffering, holding instead to the more secular Greek philosophical mindset. This mindset in turn compelled them to seek answers to life, suffering and evil—and Christianity came as the perfect fit: it proposed solid answers through reason and faith, disciplines in which Roman world was immersed. Westernization became the assured result of Christianity's spread, for even though its origins and thinking were thoroughly Eastern, its theology eventually became the essence of the West.

Inside Information

The identity of the West as *the West* took shape during the centuries-long advance of Christian evangelism and Christendom—especially under the Emperor Constantine, who legalized Christianity and encouraged its ideas about evil and suffering to affect the late Roman Empire from uninhibited Biblical influences. This act shaped the thinking processes of the Western world: when something "bad" happened, the Western mind defaulted to a dual mode of reasoning—the first, an immediate appraisal of the situation according to historical Christian moral and ethical teachings. The second pored over the fairness or justness of the event, again measured by longstanding Biblical principles.

These two approaches are hardly unique to Christianized

thinking and culture, as they are universally and inherently understood (as mentioned earlier). But a remarkable distinction lies at the core of Christian belief—namely that God has deliberately etched His definitive laws of right and wrong on the human conscience, so that every living person possesses a natural discernment of what is good and what is evil.

Even more striking, until the first missionary journeys of the early church, only those living in and around the Jewish enclaves scattered throughout the Gentile-dominated Roman Empire (or anywhere else, for that matter) had any knowledge whatsoever of the Ten Commandments, the writings of Moses and of Biblical teachings about good and evil. Yet even the ancient Gentiles understood the same basic measure of right, wrong, good and evil as both the religious Jews of that age and the modern inhabitants of today's world.

It was in this light that the Apostle Paul wrote in his letter to the church at Rome, "Indeed, when Gentiles, who do not have the law, do by nature things required by the law, they are a law for themselves, even though they do not have the law, since they show that the requirements of the law are written on their hearts, their consciences also bearing witness, and their thoughts now accusing, now even defending them."[xlvi]

As he languished in a freezing Soviet gulag, Nobel laureate Alexander Solzhenitsyn gradually awoke to the unavoidable reality of this phenomenon. He later wrote, "It was only when I lay there on the rotting prison straw that I sensed within myself the first stirrings of good. Gradually, it was disclosed to me that the line separating good and evil passes not between states nor between social classes nor between political parties, but right through every human heart, through all human hearts. And that is why I turn back to the years of my imprisonment and say, sometimes to the astonishment of those about me, *bless you, prison, for having been a part of my life.*[xlvii] [Emphasis in the original]

Even more, it follows that all goodness is somehow perfectly in line with God's nature, and all evil entirely contradictory of it. C.S. Lewis concluded,

> "We have two bits of evidence about the Somebody [the divine source of the instinctive moral law]. One is the universe He has made…[t]he other…is that Moral Law which He has put into our minds. And this is a better bit of evidence than the other, because it is inside information. You find out more about God from the Moral Law than from the universe in general just as you find out more about a man by listening to his conversation than by looking at a house he has built. Now, from this second bit of evidence we conclude that the Being behind the universe is intensely interested in right conduct—in fair play, unselfishness, courage, good faith, honesty and truthfulness. In that sense we should

agree with the account given by Christianity and some other religions, that God is 'good.'"[xlviii]

The Western view of evil springs from this universal, unlearned understanding described, but not defined, in Paul's letter to the Romans.

Why the World is a Mess

Hinduism and Buddhism suggest that the world should never have been, while secularism argues that the world was a cosmic accident. But the Bible proposes that the world should have been something other than what it is.[xlix] This radical distinction not only sets apart Judeo-Christianity from virtually all other philosophical and religious systems—it is the bedrock of its understanding of the problem of suffering and evil. In fact, to the Judeo-Christian, it is the key to hope.

The Bible assigns to the Devil both the first expression of evil in the history of eternity and the ultimate source of universal evil and suffering. The Biblical account of the Fall of Man in the Garden of Eden was the cataclysmic crossroad in time and space when God's perfect, unbroken creation was, through a masterstroke of deceit, handed over to Satan's ruinous intentions. According to the Bible, original evil took root in the prideful heart of the exalted cherub Lucifer, who bent all his considerable will against God. Following his expulsion from God's presence and through a cunning lie, he awakened in innocent Adam and Eve a similar sense of pride and self-glorification, dooming the cosmos. As a result, God's perfect creation became broken and cursed.

Man, duped into the pursuit of a self-oriented spiritual supremacy, rebelled against his Creator, bringing death and suffering into the once perfect realm. Because of his blatant aspiration to personal divinity, God gave man over to his own nefarious desires, crowning him as master of a world that he was determined to dominate. In effect, God handed man the title deed to the earth, who by default conceded it to Satan. The world became shattered and cursed—but it was never meant to be like that. In the words of Os Guinness, "It ought to have been otherwise."

The Apostle Paul, in his letter to the church at Rome, described how humanity would be bound to endure the wrath of God on earth because of its deliberate and ongoing rebellion against Him:

> "The wrath of God is being revealed from heaven against all the godlessness and wickedness of men who suppress the truth by their wickedness, since what may be known about God is plain to them, because God has made it plain to them. For since the creation of the world God's invisible qualities— his eternal power and divine nature—have been clearly seen, being understood from what has been made, so that men are without excuse. For although

they knew God, they neither glorified him as God nor gave thanks to him, but their thinking became futile and their foolish hearts were darkened. Although they claimed to be wise, they became fools and exchanged the glory of the immortal God for images made to look like mortal man and birds and animals and reptiles."[1]

In other words, man is under wrath not because God is a cruel and fickle tyrant, but because mankind deliberately and foolishly rejected Him as both Creator and Lord. Paul further explains,

"Therefore God gave them over in the sinful desires of their hearts to sexual impurity for the degrading of their bodies with one another. They exchanged the truth of God for a lie, and worshiped and served created things rather than the Creator—who is forever praised. Amen. Because of this, God gave them over to shameful lusts. Even their women exchanged natural relations for unnatural ones. In the same way the men also abandoned natural relations with women and were inflamed with lust for one another. Men committed indecent acts with other men, and received in themselves the due penalty for their perversion. Furthermore, since they did not think it worthwhile to retain the knowledge of God, he gave them over to a depraved mind, to do what ought not to be done. They have become filled with every kind of wickedness, evil, greed and depravity. They are full of envy, murder, strife, deceit and malice. They are gossips, slanderers, God-haters, insolent, arrogant and boastful; they invent ways of doing evil; they disobey their parents; they are senseless, faithless, heartless, ruthless. Although they know God's righteous decree that those who do such things deserve death, they not only continue to do these very things but also approve of those who practice them."[li]

It was here that the Apostle Paul exposed the foundation of the Judeo-Christian view—the Western view—of the problem of evil and suffering in the world. His description was not of the apocalyptic Wrath to Come, which will happen at the end of the world. This was a wrath with a small 'w,' the wrath of God revealed *now*, against "the godlessness and wickedness of men." It was a wrath into which the world has been immersed since man's catastrophic fall in the Garden of Eden, one that he must endure until the physical return of Jesus Christ.

But it is not a wrath of brimstone and wasting plague. It is a wrath where rebellious humanity has, as a species, been given over by God to its own will and desires. In other words, the evil and suffering in the world is not a result of God's inability to defeat villainy and alleviate affliction—rather, it is His vivid demonstration to the world of the *best* man can do as the god he is so determined to become.

A theology student observed, "Man, when left to natural unmitigated impulses, will use all manner of contrivances to succeed or exact revenge upon others. In fact, most of human suffering can probably be attributed to this source. It is humans, not God, who have fashioned guns, bombs, whips, torture chambers, disease and genocide. Indeed, it is primarily by human greed and languor that we have poverty."[lii]

Dr. Peter Kreeft noted, "Built into the situation of God deciding to create human beings is the chance of evil and, consequently, the suffering that results…The source of evil is not God's power but mankind's freedom…The overwhelming majority of pain in the world is caused by our choices to kill, to slander, to be selfish, to stray sexually, to break our promises, to be reckless."[liii] Dr. Norman Geisler's bearing on the issue is perhaps the most laconic: "God made evil possible and subsequently men make evil actual."[liv]

"Experience the Power of You!"[lv] proclaimed the cheery motto of a popular national media corporation. Ironically, the world has been experiencing exactly that—along with all the fruit of its own misbegotten authority. Moreover, man, seeing himself as his own god, indicts himself as he accuses God for the evil in the world, for he is only observing the reflection of his own feeble, fanciful sovereignty. Man is looking into the mirror of himself. Humanity was simply given over by God to its own will and ways, and the evil and suffering of the world was the assured result. God did not make things the way they are. Man did. *This is the Hurricane.*

Even more, an underlying theme permeating every book of the Bible is the fact that all people suffer and all people die. Most of the Psalms concern personal or national suffering, as do most of the decrees of the Old Testament prophets. The Children of Israel suffered for hundreds of years and on multiple occasions in brutal bondage. An entire generation of them, numbering well over a million, died off as they wandered the wastelands of Arabia on their forty-year journey to the Promised Land.

The people of the Bible—God's people—were starved, conquered by enemies, ruled by tyrants, enslaved and deported. Husbands lost wives and wives husbands. Mothers lost babies, and children were stricken with disease or slaughtered by invaders. Kings, prophets, patriarchs, priests, generals, apostles, villains, heroes, peasants, slaves, benefactors, young and old—God's chosen people all—every one of them suffered and eventually died or was slain, including God's only begotten Son Jesus Christ. Yet it remains even among Western thinking people that death and suffering somehow ought not to be, especially for *me* and *the ones I love.* And when it strikes, surely God must be unfair and cruel. It is here where answers begin to emerge out of the darkness.

Professor Peter Kreeft observed,

"What do the myths and dreams say about the mystery of suffering and the two associated mysteries of death and injustice (bad things happening to good people)? Essentially the same thing as the familiar story in Genesis. They say something almost no one in the world but orthodox Jews and Christians believe any more: that suffering and death and injustice all came into the world late, by a fall, or fault, or accident on our part; that we were originally innocent, happy and immortal; that we brought suffering into the world; that we remember paradise lost."[lvi]

This is the essence of a person's pain and how he is able to identify evil as evil. *It should not have happened, but it did, and it happened to me or to my loved one, and it hurts beyond all measure.*

Such an anguished cry erupts from real pain, but it is also an affirmation of the real condition of the world according to the Bible. The blame for suffering is almost always hurled back at God, and understandably so, yet He was not the cause, and He has told us so. The Scriptures make it clear that all people will suffer and die. Period. It was not meant to be that way, and it will not always be that way, but for this age of the world God has told us that it must be. To put it another way, God did not tell people they would *not* suffer and die, in fact, quite to the contrary. What He *did* reveal to humanity is that He is able to intervene, heal, provide and defeat Satan as long as it is in His will and purposes to do so.

This is a tremendous truth—but it is also a fragile one if left there. Why? Every person who was ever miraculously healed or set free from some devilish bondage has eventually died, and every person God raised from the dead lived only to die again (with the unique exception of Jesus). God is able to help, but He has also made it clear that His intervention will be at His sovereign discretion. Further, regardless of the form of His response to their prayers, people are commanded to utterly submit to His will while petitioning Him for relief. This certainly seems cold and almost cruelly aloof, especially coming from one so irresistibly powerful and able to make a difference.

What then is the solution to the problem? God has *not* promised that people would *not* suffer, experience evil or die. But the God of the Bible is acting in perfect accordance with what He said He would do. He is acting in *truth*. And He also promised that He *understands* the sufferer's plight—thoroughly and from the inside out—that He is there, and will faithfully stand with the afflicted, dispossessed and dying throughout their terrible ordeal. This is compassion, mercy and love at its most transcendent, shining out in a world of darkness and suffering—in a world of man's making. *This is the Eye of the Hurricane.*

An Unfortunate Trend

Both the modern world and post-modernism have taken a toll on the Western view of evil. It has become increasingly routine for prosperous, healthy people to snub the idea of objective evil and the next moment curse it when they are crushed beneath some senseless suffering. Such thinking is typical of the average Westerner where, as long as it is convenient to believe one thing, one need not regard another, less agreeable idea until forced to do so. And even then, its truth is wrestled with and vigorously opposed.

When confronted with tragedy, the fictional Scarlet O'Hara of *Gone with the Wind* would wall off her agony with the naïve motto, "I can't think about that now. I'll think about that tomorrow…" Interestingly, her words have proven quite prophetic. This is an unfortunate trend in the West, for in a culture rich with good medicine, abundant food and clean water, ready welfare and disaster services, trustworthy policing and an unrivaled prosperity, the inevitability of evil and personal suffering remains ominously undiminished. In fact, the average thriving Westerner will one day require comfort, compassion and answers as desperately as a destitute orphan begging in the muddy streets of Bangladesh. The question is, where will they turn? Who can hold out *genuine* hope, healing, purpose, courage and reason?

"All that we call human history—money, poverty, ambition, war, prostitution, classes, empires, slavery—is the long terrible story of man trying to find something other than God for which to make him happy."

—C.S. Lewis

"No man chooses evil because it is evil; he only mistakes it for happiness, the good he seeks."

—Mary Wollstonecraft

SO WHAT?

Of the world's three main families of faith, when you honestly examine their ideas about God, truth, good, evil and hope, two are sorely lacking.

The Eastern offers fatalistic frustration, supplying no answers, no aspirations and no realistic break from an endless, agonizing cycle of life, death and rebirth. Obviously sorely lacking.

The Secular exercises an enormous degree of pretense, declaring that reason and science have given the human species purpose and meaning in an accidental universe—one that will eventually kill us all and leave nothing behind; not even a memory. Obviously sorely lacking.

Christianity, on the other hand, stands alone as the only understanding of God that answers all of these questions with hope and destiny. More than that, it does not offer comfort and compassion in spite of what it believes, *but because of it*.

Os Guinness puts it like this:

"Where else are we to go? Which other faith comes close to matching the biblical answer for its combination of realism, hope and courage? Buddhism, for example, has been described as the most radical 'No' to human aspirations ever formulated. And while I personally have sometimes admired the nobility of great atheists I have met such as Bertrand Russell, there is a bleakness to the nobility that is almost unendurable. 'Atheism,' in the words of Jean Paul Sartre, 'is a cruel long-term business, and I have gone through it to the end.' In contrast to all such views, the gospel is truly the best news ever, with its prospect of a world in which evil and suffering are gone, justice and peace are restored, and the very last tear is wiped away."[lvii]

Following the 2005 Hurricane Katrina disaster, former Parliament member and radical atheist, Roy Hattersley, made an uncharacteristic admission about the many aid groups involved in the relief efforts. The self-described "unrepentant atheist" observed that virtually all of the groups had "a religious origin and character." What is more, Hattersley acknowledged that,

"Notable by their absence [were] teams from rationalist societies, free thinkers' clubs, and atheists' associations—the sort of people who not only scoff at religion's intellectual absurdity but also regard it as a positive force of evil.... The only possible conclusion is that faith comes with a packet of moral imperatives that, while they do not condition the attitude of all believers, influence enough of them to make them morally superior to atheists like me. The truth may make us free. But it has not made us admirable as the average captain in the Salvation Army."

His article was entitled, *Faith Does Breed Charity: We atheists have to accept that most believers are better human beings.*[lviii]

Part Four

TRUTH IS TRUTH

"Grace fills empty spaces, but it can only enter where there is a void to receive it, and it is grace itself which makes this void…To accept a void in ourselves is supernatural."

—Simone Weil

"God whispers to us in our pleasures, speaks in our conscience, but shouts in our pains; it is His megaphone to rouse a deaf world."

—C.S. Lewis

THE BASIS OF ALL COMFORT

"One word of truth shall outweigh the whole world."

—Russian proverb

To ease the effects of evil and suffering, compassion and answers must have a foundation of truth that is *true*. Like a mathematical problem, to balance the equation of life and suffering, factors of unchanging truth and value are essential, or things will simply not add up. Without solid truth, genuine compassion and answers are traded for the slush of platitudes and sentiments. For the sufferer seeking comfort and the one who offers it, only truth will do.

The secularist solution to evil and suffering lies in the scientific and the therapeutic. By outlawing the spiritual, however, neither is really capable of ministering to a person's soul or spirit, the existence of which secularism also disputes. Further, the secularist offerings of hope and purpose are by nature dishonest, because they seek to assign meaning in a universe in which none can be established. Nietzsche understood the severity of the problem, declaring that in a rational, God-rejecting world, "Hope is the worst of evils, for it prolongs the torment of man."[lix]

If this is so, then offering hope where none really exists and aspiration in the face of extinction would be handing the sufferer a rainbow—a lovely, shining thing without substance, its pot of golden truth forever lost in the land of leprechauns. Moreover, if there is no true evil (as secularism suggests), then comfort and compassion inspired by human sympathy and empathy may indeed offer psychological remedies—but to what end? Will all be well one day? Will all be well one day *forever*? If that is the true condition of the world, then it is impossible—and to suggest otherwise would be at best clichéd and ignorant.

Simply put, to attempt to provide comfort from a secular position to someone who has been torn by evil may be a noble, very human thing, but to offer hope and a future would be as arbitrary as a flip of a coin.

Auschwitz survivor and psychiatrist Viktor Frankl concluded that hopelessness ought to be countered with the understanding that no matter what is happening today, "tomorrow is waiting." Frankl's optimism is positively enlightened, and such an idea amounts to all but a Biblical axiom. When applied in a secularist context his premise can only carry a person as far as their deathbed, at which time all such altruism dissolves.[6]

The Eastern view presents its own difficulties—it is

---

[6] Frankl was a Progressive (generally agnostic) Jew, and thus largely secularist in his thinking.

brutally realistic concerning evil and suffering, but it is also resigned to its own hopeless and endless karmic cycles. According to the clockwork of its vast philosophical tenets, whatever is considered *true* is the *now* dictated by karma, and to which all people are held hostage, world without end. While this Eastern view can provide a certain measure of objectivity and absolutism, it lacks the mandate for compassion or the will to furnish it. One's place in the universe is *one's place*—why should someone interfere or intercede?

Further, if the universe is so uncertain as to be the dream of a sleeping god, then what is the substance of reality? And what would be the place of others? Would anyone or anything actually matter? It was Jesus who taught His disciples to deny themselves in order to make life better for others, not the Buddha, who taught that there is no self (despite the paradoxical Buddhist idea that one's self must be eliminated). Christian apologist Dr. Ravi Zacharias observed that, "when a person cries, self is proven *real*... [Suffering, therefore,] is not a problem of pain, but the essence of being."[lx]

And here's the big rub: The Eastern view of suffering and evil offers people a set of fuzzy figures and values to balance the equation—or none at all. Regardless of the nature of the proposition, when calculated, the historical accounting has consistently produced a null set.

And then there is that third view...

ANSWERING THE UNANSWERABLE

"Without truth there is only manipulation."

—Os Guinness

Not even Western Judeo-Christianity can answer every question aimed at the problem of evil and suffering. Even so, it's not hard to see that it proposes the most rational, albeit narrow claim to absolute truth, especially when it comes to measurable compassion and others-centeredness demonstrated by Jesus of Nazareth.

Yet Christians still suffer and die, and many will question God only to be answered with an apparent and painful silence. Some may brand questioning God as doubt or irreverence, and therefore sinful or worse. Such self-reproof, however, is as unwarranted as it is itself sinful. To the contrary, Dr. Peter Kreeft observed, "We doubt. Doubt is glorious. Only one who can doubt can believe, just as only one who can despair can hope, and only one who can hate can love."[lxi]

Even more, those who claim to possess all (or none) of the answers to the challenge of evil and suffering demonstrate a lack of appreciation of the value of questions. Dr. Kreeft adds,

> "Questioning is equally far removed from both dogmatism (thinking you have all the answers) and skepticism (believing there are no answers). Neither the dogmatist nor the skeptic questions. Dogmatism is intellectual pride and skepticism is intellectual despair; they are equal and opposite extremes, like pride and despair in the moral sphere. Questioning, therefore, is opposed to pride. No one should ever discourage questioning, whether in themselves or in another. Jesus always respected his disciples' questions, no matter how foolish they were. Parents, teachers, or preachers who discourage questioning are acting like dogmatists or skeptics; they are either arrogant or cowardly, prideful or despairing."[lxii]

And the same is true for us.

The Judeo-Christian view lays out a decidedly narrow and non-negotiable view of truth, yet its logic is rational, its devotees are (mostly) dedicated and others-centered and its claim to divine revelation unbendable. The question is how can such an unyielding truth be compassionately applied to someone deeply afflicted?

The answer to this question is quite obvious when you think about it. Such truth can be offered on its own merit because it is inherently right and good. In other words, the genuineness of such truth is shown in selfless, compassionate acts done not because it is the Christian thing to do, but because it is the *right* thing to do. Os Guinness put it like this:

> "[T]he Christian faith is not true because it works; it works because it is true. It is not true because we experience it; we experience it—deeply and gloriously—because it is true. It is not simply 'true for us'; it is true for any who seek in order to find, because truth is true even if nobody believes it and falsehood is false even if everybody believes it. That is why truth does not yield to opinion, fashion, numbers, office, or sincerity—it is simply true and that is the end of it."[lxiii]

An answer that is not true is no answer. It might be a placebo spoken by a compassionate person who has nothing substantial to say. It could be a platitude—a canned word from a helper who is too proud to admit that he just doesn't know. Or it might be a lie—a vapory fabrication pointing to a hope where none exists.

If answers to the problem of evil and suffering are not truth-based, how could they ever qualify as real answers? They have to be more than theory—they must be self-evident, because truth is the place where words and actions intersect. Truth without compassion is harsh, even brutal; compassion without truth is sloppy sentimentality, lacking the authority of genuine goodness. To offer baseless hopes, philosophical platitudes or religious resignation to a suffering person may be the greatest evil of all, even worse than doing nothing.

In order for it to be real and compassionate, truth *cannot* be relative, and it *must* be objective. To withhold objectivity or offer a compassionate non-truth is tantamount to a lie, making the endeavor wholly uncompassionate—and perhaps harmful.

A DRASTIC PROPOSITION

"There comes a moment when the children who have been playing burglars hush suddenly: was that a real footstep in the hall? There comes a moment when people who have been dabbling in religion...suddenly draw back. Supposing we really found Him? We never meant it to come to that! Worse still, supposing He had found us?"

—C.S. Lewis

Buddhists, Hindus, atheists and agnostics of all sorts are more than capable of offering tremendous kindness and compassion, for we are all human and we understand our human need for comfort and consolation. Even so, at this point it seems reasonable to propose an idea that is both sweeping and (to some) scandalous: *truthful* compassion and *truthful* answers to suffering and evil are not possible apart from the Judeo-Christian standard.

Think about it—by virtue of their own stated philosophical principles, the Eastern and Secular models generally lack an inner consistency shaped by an objective reality. This is a drastic proposition, for in an increasingly relativistic and "tolerant" world, who would dare assert that *their* moral and spiritual system is truer than that of others?

Star Trek creator Gene Roddenberry boldly declared, "Those who insist theirs is the only correct government or economic system deserve the same contempt as those who insist that they have the only true God."[lxiv] Despite the glaring double standard in his statement, millions today hold fast to the same toothless philosophical credo: that there is no absolute truth except the truth that there is no absolute truth.[lxv]

But if there is no absolute truth and everything must be viewed without boundaries and bias, then Roddenberry's indictment contains no more substance than any other system of belief. On the other hand, if someone, somewhere is actually *right*, such truth would have to be *narrow*, because truth, by its absolute nature, is *extremely* narrow. On that basis alone, Christianity becomes an obvious contender as the cornerstone of objective authority.

Both the Eastern and Secular families of faith traditionally balk at objectivity, showing indifference and even resistance to the idea of absolutes. As a result, both deny the moral and philosophical authority to genuinely address the cries of hurting people. On the other hand, the historical Jesus of Nazareth frequently claimed to possess absolute authority in His words and deeds.

This vexing possibility has provoked many to try to redefine Christ in order to make Him and his radical teachings less challenging and His remaining sayings more benign. But efforts to reinvent Jesus tend to break down because logically, objectivity is not subject to subjectivity. Even more, Jesus not only made radical statements about His universal authority and personal divinity, His claims were validated by His miracles, His unrivaled words and by His physical resurrection from the dead, all of which were extensively witnessed and reported.

C.S. Lewis came to appreciate the extraordinary authority of Christianity to provide comfort that was indissolubly integrated with truth. He wrote:

> "Of course, I quite agree that the Christian religion
> is, in the long run, a thing of unspeakable comfort…
> If you look for truth, you may find comfort in the
> end: if you look for comfort you will not get either
> comfort or truth—only soft soap and wishful
> thinking to begin with and, in the end, despair."[lxvi]

As comforters, we are driven by compassion itself to uphold the integrity of truth as we mete out comfort, answers to evil and hope, for truth is the fundamental element of compassion,

ANSWERING EVIL

and compassion must be an agent of truth.

The Apostle John told his readers that, "grace and truth came through Jesus Christ." This is a crucial combination of words, because grace without truth is meaningless and truth without grace can be brutal. What other system of belief suggests a ministry that is gentler in tenderness, graceful in honesty, hopeful in purpose and powerful to attend to a turbulent, shattered heart?

This is the bedrock of effective compassion, but it is a salve that must be applied carefully and with grace, lest it prove as brutal as the evil itself.

99

UNNATURAL

"Death is natural."

"Dying is merely a part of living."

"Dying is a natural process, it is a beautiful thing."

I'm sure you've heard those sayings before. They are familiar, time-honored platitudes that are frequently (if not tenderly) doled out by well-meaning people who are not quite sure what to say to a bereaved person. I have also heard the same banalities offered by ministers, chaplains, caregivers and therapists—yet few expressions have proven less beneficial or further from the truth. In fact, trying to package the mind-numbing heartbreak of bereavement by reducing death to the natural order of things is neither healing nor compassionate. The torment of human loss is, in fact, *anything but* natural, which is why its impact is so utterly devastating. Let me explain...

On a breezy spring afternoon I received an urgent call informing me that a dear friend, a retired truck driver and mountain of a man, had suffered a sudden aneurism that rendered him brain-dead. When I arrived at the hospital, I discovered my friend's grown daughter standing vigil at his bedside. Her face was red and tear-stained, her swollen eyes and clenched teeth bore a mixed expression of confusion and rage. Still clutching her father's naked foot, her outrage erupted as I approached.

"This is all wrong!" she cried.

"Yes, it is—it is horribly wrong," I said.

Within seconds her hard countenance softened and her rigid shoulders loosened and drooped.

"It is?" she replied, stunned by my response. "I didn't think you, of all people, would say such a thing. It's *wrong*?"

It was, and it was not simply that the circumstances felt bad. To the grieving daughter my unexpected agreement confirmed to her what she—and nearly everyone—suspected despite all the sentiments to the contrary: death was *unnatural*. Yes, it was common to life, but it was wrong, it was evil, it was an *enemy*. For the first time in her life (and to her relief) her guarded suspicions were verified.

Natural is a convenient word often used to pigeonhole a tragic situation, due in part to its vast and hazy definition. Signifying neither good nor evil, *natural* only affirms a tragedy's existence and inevitability.

That's the way it is—it will just have to be lived with.

To suggest that death is *natural* is also morally vague and quite fitting to the secularistic ideal. Regardless of one's system of belief, however, it is apparent that lurking in every human heart is an understanding that death is somehow a great evil and horrendously wrong—an inherent knowledge that, somehow, *it should not have been this way.*

In his book, *Unspeakable,* Dr. Os Guinness highlights a familiar incident in the Gospel of John that holds a surprising revelation of the Christian view of death and bereavement. In John's account, by the time Jesus of Nazareth arrived at Lazarus' house, His dear friend had already been dead and buried four days. As Jesus approached, he was met by Lazarus' bereaved sisters, both of whom lodged the same complaint: "Lord, if you had only been here, my brother would not have died." What John recorded next was both vital and shattering:

> When Jesus saw [Lazarus' sister Mary of Bethany] weeping, and the Jews who had come along with her also weeping, he was deeply moved in his spirit and troubled. "Where have you laid him?" he asked. "Come and see, Lord," they replied. Jesus wept.[lxvii]

This emotional passage is famous for the intimate implications of those two last words. But just as significant was John's observation, "he was deeply moved in his spirit and troubled." As Dr. Guinness points out, that expression does not translate well into English, but its usage in the passage indicates that Jesus was not just moved, He was outraged—even furious. In fact, the Greek tragedian, Aeschylus, used the same term to describe warhorses "rearing up on their hind legs, snorting through their nostrils, and charging into battle."[lxviii]

But at what or whom was Jesus so angry? At the sisters and the visiting mourners? Was he upset with their apparent doubt of Him and his abilities? The context hints at something much more personal to Jesus. The Son of God, Guinness suggests, was brought face to face with the tragic death of one of His closest friends knowing that it was all so terribly wrong—that the world should have been otherwise. He did not want things to be so, and He came into the world to change everything. But as the Apostle Paul reminded his readers, the very last enemy to be destroyed would be death, which had once again won the day.

To suggest to a grieving survivor that their tragedy is just the natural order of things is to ignore a greater spiritual truth. On the other hand, to tell someone that their dreadful loss is simply the unsearchable will of a sovereign God—though true—is only half the story. That a person died of a God-ordained beating or was murdered by a sovereign gun demands that we submit to the divine providence of the crime and set about recovering from the pain of it. But death *infuriated* Jesus because it was *not* His will—the world was *not* made to be this way—the good and exquisite creation of God was in ruins.

Even though Jesus was about to miraculously revive his dead friend, His reaction to the tragedy was severe. He saw death for the evil it really was. The world of His perfect creation lay shattered and broken before His eyes; death was reigning as a relentless and brutal enemy, and He, more than any other, could see it with perfect clarity: *it should have been otherwise*.

If we grasp this concept, we hold a tremendous truth that can free a grieving survivor. Os Guinness, who buried two brothers in the mission field of China, concluded:

> "Once you know in the depth of your soul that the world should have been otherwise, you are free to feel what it is human to feel: sorrow at what is heartbreaking, shock at what is shattering, and outrage at what is flagrantly wrong and out of joint. Indeed, it is every bit as wrong not to be angry when we should be as to be angry when we should not be. To pretend otherwise is to be too pious by half, and harder on ourselves than Jesus himself was."[lxix]

It ought to have been otherwise, and Jesus Christ is in perfect agreement, for only Christianity has a cross, and, as Dr. Guinness observed, "No other god has wounds."

As she languished in the chambers of the Nazi death camp

Ravensbrook, Corrie Ten Boom confessed, "This darkness is very deep, but our God has gone deeper still." It is this radiant truth that allows us to grieve with the comforting realization that God grieves with us.

HORRENDOUS

"After Auschwitz there is no God; after Mauthausen there is no morality; after Treblinka there is no sense."

—Bob Brecher

— Caution: Disturbing Content —

Late on the evening of June 14, 2008, twenty-seven-year-old Sergio Aguilar got out of his car in the middle of a rural Stanislaus County road and began to viciously stomp on his toddler son. When the police arrived, Aguilar, now held at gunpoint, calmly explained that he "had to get the demons out of him," and continued his horrifying assault. Aguilar was immediately shot dead by the officers and the baby was pronounced deceased at the scene, damaged beyond recognition. The act was unspeakably hideous, and the motive, in the end, irrelevant. Two people lay dead, one wholly innocent and good, the other a human monstrosity who perpetrated an act that blasphemed his natural role as a father. That same day in various unnamed places around the world, other ordinary men and women committed hundreds, if not thousands of similar brutalities on innocent people.

Everyone dies, but it should have been otherwise; God told us it would happen, and He stands by His Word. But where was He when this little toddler was brutally murdered?

The Holocaust, the killing fields of Cambodia, the Rwandan genocide and the Gulags of the Soviet Union are but a few of the countless bloodstained shrines to humanity's dreadful capacities. Huddled at the foot of these monuments are the dismayed masses who reel in grief and bewilderment, crying, "How could such things be?" Soon, however, the question shifts from rhetoric to reproach: "Who did this? There must be justice!" But to their horror the perpetrators were found to be human like the rest of us, except for what they did. "To accuse them is to condemn ourselves, for they are also us," they coldly reason. "God must be to blame—yes, we did these things, but if God *really* loved us, why did He not stop us from doing our evil?"

The charge is searing, real and illogical, but not surprising. It is also revealing. When people blame God for the misery of their own horrors, the extent of man's depravity becomes flagrant. *Where was God? Why did He allow this to happen? Could He not have prevented this?* It has been historically convenient, if not customary to point the finger at God, while the real offender has remained at large.

C.S. Lewis framed the problem like this:

"'If God were good, He would wish to make His creatures perfectly happy, and if God were almighty, He would be able to do what He wished. But the creatures are not happy. Therefore, God lacks either goodness, or power, or both.' This is the problem of pain, in its simplest form. The possibility of answering it depends on showing that the terms 'good' and 'almighty,' and perhaps also the term 'happy' are equivocal: for it must be admitted from the outset that if the popular meanings attached to these words are the best, or the only possible, meanings, then the argument is unanswerable."[lxx]

This is typical of man's reasoning, and it is sensible—but the missing piece remains objective truth, especially as God has laid it out in the Bible. Remember, because of his insistence for self-will, man was given over to sinful desires, shameful lusts and depravity of mind. Further, God openly declared His just decision and subsequent actions in the matter.[lxxi] So the question is not "Could not God have prevented these things?" but rather, "Why is He obligated to do so?" In fact, He explained to us exactly what He did with humanity—He gave him over to his own will.

Yet, like a spoiled child, man insists on immunity from the consequences of his wrong-headedness and blames the parent. God is innocent, holy and incapable of evil, and He has proven Himself utterly truthful by doing precisely what He said He would do. This, in turn, verifies His relentless love for humanity throughout its rebellious history. God is just, so He has placed mankind under wrath because of our blatant self-will. But God is also *there*, because He said He would be—*always*—especially for those who call upon Him, and even for those who never would.

"If these things are true about God," someone may say, "then where was He when my world came crashing down? Where was He when I wept and wailed all night? Where is His promised comfort and presence? I certainly don't feel anything from Him!"

Most of us have heard cries like this, and perhaps you have even felt the same way. The answer to such agonized inquiries is almost child-like in its simplicity, yet extremely difficult because it defies rationality. The answer lies just on the other side of a door called faith. This is no cop-out: God told the truth—now it is time to believe Him.

We who serve in the eye of the storm hold the key to this door, but all we can do is unlock it. There is a powerful ray of light shining through the keyhole, but the victim has to open it. For most people it's not the creaky wooden door of an old church, but the heavy iron door of a vault—they know something valuable is inside, but it will take enormous effort to pull it open.

It is here we become coaches. We encourage and pray, but our hands are tied by the will of the victim—and though most hurting people want to open the door, it remains to be seen if they will ever try. It is also here where the sorrow of one person will become the joy—or the heartbreak of both.

TOUGH QUESTIONS, HARD ANSWERS

"We just don't want to embrace the God who can be found in the midst of pain. We'd rather listen to Jesus preach sweet sermons about lilies."
—Joni Eareckson Tada

Everyone dies, but it should have been otherwise—God told us it will happen, and He stands by His Word. Even so, where *was* God when that little toddler was savagely murdered? Why did He allow it to happen? Could He not have prevented this?

Yes, He could have.

Why, then, did the almighty, loving, compassionate, merciful God just let it happen?

That is not the right question. He said such evil would happen, and that for it not to occur would be inconsistent with what He declared in the Bible.

But why should an innocent child die under the filthy boots

of a murderous father? Was he also a horrible sinner like his killer?

Obviously not.

Was he innocent?

Completely.

Does God love the little children?

Of course He does, and He told us so.

Then was it God's cold retribution for another's sin? And, while we're on the subject, how could "the glory of God" be displayed in the brutal murder of a child?

Tough questions.

Jesus was constantly battered with tough questions—and He had the right answers. Seeing a blind man, His disciples asked Him, "Rabbi, who sinned, this man or his parents that he was born blind?" "Neither," replied Jesus, "but this happened so that the work of God might be displayed in his life."[lxxii] Another time Jesus was asked about the reason for a recent tragedy that occurred in Jerusalem. He responded, "...those eighteen who died when the tower of Siloam fell on them—do you think they were more guilty than all the others living in Jerusalem? I tell you, no!"[lxxiii]

But how could God's goodness be found in the brutal murder of a child? The Bible does not command hurting people to embrace evil or suggest that they should somehow grow to appreciate it—God *hates* evil, and He expects no less passion about it from us. Everything God does is good, but despite His sovereignty, the Bible is also clear that not everything is done by God.

What happened was bad—horrendously so, and evil—and God is in perfect agreement. God *hates* murder, war, genocide, persecution, plague, disease, injustice, bigotry, child-abuse, torture, horrific accidents, terror attacks, cancer, insanity and the like. In fact, such atrocities provoke His fury. The larger question remains, however: how could God bring any good whatsoever out of such appalling evil? The answer, in this case, may not come to us in this life.

A young pastor who suffered a disabling stroke once told me: "There are some things in this world that defy any explanation—not just of human behavior, but of God's ultimate dealings with us in the midst of that behavior. Not everything 'works together for the good…' —at least not to our eyes."

Perhaps French philosopher and social activist Simone Weil said it best: "The extreme greatness of Christianity lies in the fact that it does not seek a supernatural cure for suffering, but a supernatural use of it."[lxxiv] She died of tuberculosis at the age of thirty-four.

CAN HE NOT...?

The Biblical book of Daniel records a collision of wills between a malignant tyrant and three of his royal advisors. The king was Nebuchadnezzar, one of the most self-possessed despots in history; his advisors were a trio of young, displaced Hebrews named Hananiah, Mishael and Azariah, more famously known as Shadrach, Meshach, and Abednego. They defied the King's threat to roast alive anyone who refused to worship his colossal golden image. Now they stood before him in judgment.

Infuriated by their boldness, King Nebuchadnezzar ranted, "If you do not worship [the idol I made], you will be thrown immediately into the blazing furnace. Then what god will be able to rescue you from my hand?"

Their reply was unyielding: "O Nebuchadnezzar, we do not need to defend ourselves before *you* in this matter. If we are thrown into the blazing furnace, *the God we serve is able* to save us from it, and He will rescue us from your hand, O king. *But even if He does not*, we want you to know, O king, that we will not serve your gods or worship the image you have set up."[lxxv] [Emphasis added]

The three young Hebrews held fast to a tremendous principle: God is *able* to deliver from any and all evil, misery and death—but *even if He does not*, they would still resist all efforts to abandon their trust in Him.

Nebuchadnezzar ordered their immediate execution. An appalling decree had been forced on a displaced people, and out of devotion to their God, three of its finest youth stood their ground. Even so, the God to whom they entrusted their lives still allowed them to be condemned to a fiery death. Could He not save them? Did He not care?

Then something unexpected happened: hurled alive into a blazing furnace, the Hebrews did not burn. And even more alarming, the astonished tyrant saw a *fourth* figure in the furnace walking with them in the flames—someone human yet otherworldly, who looked to him "like a son of the gods." Although God was able to deliver them He refused to do so, choosing instead to personally accompany the captives into their terrible ordeal.

Deliverance from evil and agony is certainly preferable to the alternative, but any divine rescue from earthly suffering is only temporary. The one who is healed today will suffer a different affliction tomorrow; the one who has been raised from the dead will live to die another day. But discovering that He stands with the afflicted in their ordeal reveals God's tender lovingkindness and faithfulness toward us all. He is always right where He promised He would be—He is *with us*, especially in the furnace of life's most searing moments. And like the three Hebrew youths, we can trust Him even as we are hurled into the flames—and when there, even more so.

Holocaust survivor Viktor Frankl discovered that in the Nazi death camps more people found and deepened their faith than lost it. He concluded that "A small and inadequate faith is like a small fire; it can be blown out by a small breeze. True faith, by contrast, is like a strong fire. When it is hit by a strong wind, it is fanned into an inextinguishable blaze."[lxxvi]

As he broke the news of his fatal liver cancer diagnosis to his stunned congregation, Pastor Jim Boice of Philadelphia's Tenth Presbyterian Church said, "The God who works miracles could have just as easily prevented this...In a fallen world, is God more glorified by preventing evil altogether or by shining in the midst of suffering? Which better demonstrates His compassion? He has told us that He has given the world over...we must expect evil to dominate until the Day of Satan's immolation; until then, including during the millennium, people will still die. The one constant is the compassionate presence of Jesus Christ."[lxxvii]

Simone Weil concluded, "The irreducible character of suffering which makes it impossible for us not to have a horror of it at the moment when we are undergoing it, is destined to bring the will to a standstill, just as absurdity brings the intelligence to a standstill, and absence love, so that man, having come to the end of his human faculties, may stretch out his arms, stop, look up and wait."[lxxviii]

A law enforcement chaplain wisely told a bereaved woman, "We must be careful not to dismiss what we *do* know about God in the face of what we *do not know*." Os Guinness noted that in the agonies of a fallen world we may never know the *why*, but we can know and can trust the God who knows why. At God's command Abraham came within seconds of sacrificing his own son as a burnt offering, and he did not know the reason why. But Abraham knew that he could trust the God who knew why. Like Abraham, we also must not forget that God is sovereign, and that in the end all will be well.[lxxix]

Why did such evil have to happen in the first place? *It did not have to*, but God warned us that it would. He also promised He would be there, closer than any man could ever be, full of perfect understanding and love. He wears the scars to prove it.

THE GREAT PURPOSE

"I…have no dread at all of the Almighty. If we ever were to meet, I should have more reproaches to make to Him than he could to me."

—Sigmund Freud, Atheist

"Why is God punishing me?" people cry—terrified that their disaster might be a divine payback for some forgotten or neglected sin. Their lament is a tormented, rhetorical reckoning of the situation—a groan that reverberates from a hollowed-out heart emptied of reason. It is a wail begging heaven to answer for a staggering injustice done where no such thing seemed justified.

"I am in agony," their mind reels, "I must have made God mad." And even though their reasoning seems confirmed by the pain, it is far from the truth of the matter.

Their sense that God is punishing them is ignited by the mingling of two volatile ingredients, namely, an overwhelmed reasoning capacity that has been exploited by the insidious whisperings of real spiritual forces intent on amplifying the torment. It is the intersection where situational evil collides with real spiritual Evil. If you find this idea offensive, you are in good company—but you may also be out of touch with the storm raging in the minds of those you seek to comfort.

On the one hand, self-blame is common to people embroiled in tragedy, often because the pain is so enormous and unnatural that it suggests some form of divine retribution. This sort of analysis is scientifically and clinically safe. The other proposition, however, suggests belief in an invisible dimension full of genuine angels and demons—an idea that many dismiss as infantile. "The *devil*?" some jeer, "Are you kidding? That's ridiculous!" But most assuredly it is not, and presumption in this arena could prove a disastrous mistake.

The Bible clearly speaks of the existence and intent of a corrupt archangel called Satan who leads a vast, malevolent army of demons. In our modern age belief in a malicious spiritual being is increasingly ridiculed as silly and culturally regressive. But even a passing glance at life and the tragedies befalling the world are much more in concert with the declarations of the Bible than with its critics.

The Bible calls Satan "the Evil One" and "the Enemy," a being with absolutely no redeeming qualities—an aspiring dark lord who would cheerfully reduce a good man to a quivering, bleeding shell, only to return and bash him again and again. He has been branded "the father of lies" and "the deceiver," titles that reveal the insidious method behind his astonishing malevolence. His unrivaled ability to persuade people to embrace heartbreaking lies may be the cruelest and most destructive weapon in his deadly arsenal.

This relentless Enemy tears at the open wounds of tragedy, injecting poisonous hints that God, who is *supposed* to be both advocate and comforter, is instead applying cold justice for some ambiguous, personal sin. And because the victim is broken and vulnerable, such lies are easily and unwittingly embraced, infecting their reeling mind with a false yet overwhelming sense of guilt.

But compounding the diabolical bashing is the occasional careless suggestion of God's punishment from a well-intentioned "helper" or, worse, a member of the clergy. This was the root of the tension between tormented Job and his so-called "comforters." "You must have done something to deserve this," they insisted. "Admit it, Job, and God may turn from His anger and like you once again!" Such comfort, however, sounds more like karma.

The result is a double-edged sword: an intense grief amplified by boorish advice and diabolical whisperings directing the victim to focus on *self*. "Why is God punishing *me*?" It is an avalanche of painful and empty introspection—a vain struggle to recall any deed on their part that would merit such a reckoning.

Worse still, piled onto the sufferer is the false and unbearable burden of self-condemnation under the crushing weight of divine contempt. Even more, the idea that "*God* must be punishing me" deprives the victim of desperately needed consolation by suggesting that God should not be approached because He is already furious with them. Such an idea is nothing short of spiritual treachery.

There is, however, another rather unsettling possibility: some tragedies may *actually be* the result of deliberate bad behavior by the survivor or victim. The age-old saying that "a man reaps what he sows" remains a Biblical axiom, and but for the grace of God, there go all of us. Needless to say, agonizing but valid feelings of guilt will inevitably accompany a tragedy that was triggered by the sufferer's bad behavior. Far more than the comfort of consolation, these people need the relief that only comes with forgiveness.

Whether our state of affairs is delightful or disastrous, according to the Bible it is all somehow sublimely purposeful:

> "All things work together for the good to those who love Him…"

> "Endure hardship as discipline, for God is treating you as sons…"

> "Consider it pure joy, my brothers, when you face trials of many kinds, because you know that the testing of your faith develops perseverance."

> "In this you greatly rejoice, though now for a little

while you may have had to suffer grief in all kinds of trials. These have come so that your faith…may be proved genuine and may result in praise, glory, and honor when Jesus Christ is revealed."

Is there a true *why*? This is the right question to ask, and the answer is not found where most expect to find it.

"Why is God punishing me?"

He is not.

"Where is He?"

Right here, with you.

"Why does He hate me?"

He does not hate you, He loves you.

"How could this be love?"

I don't know.

"Then is God against me?"

No, He is not.

"Then what am I to do?"

That is not the right question.

Here are the right questions:

If God is for us, who can be against us?

He who did not spare His own Son, but gave Him

up for us all—how will He not also, along with Him, graciously give us all things?

Who will bring any charge against those whom God has chosen? It is God who justifies.

Who is he that condemns? Christ Jesus, who died— more than that, who was raised to life—is at the right hand of God and is also interceding for us.

Who shall separate us from the Love of Christ? Shall trouble or hardship or persecution or famine or nakedness or danger or sword? As it is written, 'For Your sake we face death all day long; we are considered as sheep to be slaughtered.'

No, in all these things we are more than conquerors through Him who loved us. For I am convinced that neither death nor life, neither angels nor demons, neither the present nor the future, nor any powers, neither height nor depth, nor anything else in all creation, will be able to separate us from the love of God that is in Christ Jesus our Lord.[lxxx]

Pastor R.A. Torrey of Moody Church in Chicago called this passage "a soft pillow for a tired heart." But there is so much more happening here.

Job, in the midst of his torment, bitterly questioned God.

When God finally appeared, He told Job, "Now I will ask *you* some questions." When the Apostle Paul wrote to the Romans about their suffering, he, too, asked questions. *If God is for us, who can be against us?* When evil is answered even with a well-framed statement, our logical minds will try to dance around it, for a statement, though powerful and true, is a small thing—a dot on a very large page called life. But a good question is bigger than the universe of the imagination.

"What kind of a God would allow such things?" The question will not go away, and it haunts us. But this, too, is not the right question—simply because it does not reveal anything. Perhaps the right question is, "What kind of God would send His own Son to die for a world full of creatures capable of such rebellion and evil?" To ask this question is to have already answered it.

There will always be questions, both heart-rending and beleaguered, but the answers are greater than the questions, because the answers *are* the questions—the *right* questions.

Though He never told questioning, complaining Job the *why* of his suffering, God left him confessing, "You asked, 'Who is this that obscures My counsel without knowledge?' Surely I spoke of things I did not understand, things too wonderful for me to know." The Apostle Paul wrote, "I consider that our present sufferings are not worth comparing with the glory that will be revealed in us."

Even more, He has promised that at the end of the world evil will be judged and banished for all eternity, and that Jesus Christ Himself will wipe away every tear. It is an intimate thing to touch the face of another.

For now, it is *we* who stand in the broad and obstinate gap between a loving, compassionate God and the relentless tide of tragedy on earth. We are the rod and staff in the Good Shepherd's hands, through which He provides comfort and guidance to those who cower in the valley of the shadow of death.

To answer for the God of such magnificent things is the essence of ministry—*your* ministry. All else is procedure, and the brittle shell of a golden core.

"I know now, Lord, why you utter no answer. You are yourself the answer. Before your face questions die away. What other answer would suffice? Only words, words; to be led out to battle against other words."

—C.S. Lewis, *Till We Have Faces*

"There, peeping among the cloud-wrack above a dark tower high up in the mountains, Sam saw a white star twinkle for a while. The beauty of it smote his heart, as he looked up out of the forsaken land, and hope returned to him. For like a shaft, clear and cold, the thought pierced him that in the end the Shadow was only a small and passing thing: there was light and high beauty for ever beyond its reach."

— J.R.R. Tolkien, *The Return of the King*

The Last Part

YOU NEED TO KNOW THIS

BLESSED LIMITATIONS

"For we cannot do anything against the truth, but only for the truth. We are glad whenever we are weak but you are strong; and our prayer is for your perfection…"

—The Apostle Paul

Aside from the Lord Jesus Christ Himself, no living man or woman is up to the task of cushioning the impact of tragedy and suffering in a world given over to its own will and wants. Stir in the meddlings of an invisible, malevolent super-being bent on the corruption of all things good and we have our work cut out for us. And as we toil amid the hurricane, we're at the mercy of our own divinely imposed limitations according to the purposes of God.

Even the Apostle Paul candidly confessed his own inadequacies: "But we have this treasure [the Gospel] in jars of clay [our fragile human bodies] to show that this all-surpassing power is from God and not from us. We are hard pressed on every side, but not crushed; perplexed, but not in despair; persecuted, but not abandoned; struck down, but not destroyed."

Our limitations are ordained, which means they are not some faithless denial of Scripture or the abilities of the Holy Spirit. They are a God-imposed agency of others-centeredness and cheerful powerlessness in the face of His loving omnipotence.

By ourselves we are all inadequate to the task. But that is also a blessing, because God planned it that way. It is His way of keeping us from repeating the Great Deception, "…you will be like God, knowing good and evil."

Our Greatest Advantage

One person may possess tremendous compassion, another shining wisdom; others might serve with selfless joy, while others speak words as if from the mouth of God Himself. But these gifts are from God, neatly wrapped packages of grace given to us to hand out to others. And although our one hand is full, the other remains empty and wanting. Even though God Himself inhabits us and we are made in His image and beholden to His written truths, we will never be divine.

We are children striving to imitate a perfect Father—our great Comforter and Counselor, the One who bought and saved our souls. And because we are heirs of such tremendous grace, we, like our Father, desire to be a fountain to others of the same refreshing compassion and healing from which we have also benefited. The problem is we are human, and like those we long to serve, we, too, are fallen creatures.

But even in this dire predicament, God Himself elegantly forces the issue. He has turned our fallenness into a living constraint that allows Him the liberty to work in our lives, and as a result, in the lives of others, too.

"Where does my help come from?" asked King David. It is not from us, for though we may have excellent qualifications we are still stuck with our glaring human limitations. In fact, we are merely the ones who are called to show up. "My help comes from the Lord, the maker of heaven and earth," David answered. But if we believe firmly in whatever training or methodologies we have amassed, that we are adequately equipped to do it all for the victim, we will never be able to do so. In fact, the one who marches broad-chested into the scene, rattling with clever devices, risks blocking the victim's view of God's face and stopping their ears to His voice.

Our limitations are not evil—in fact, they are ordained and deliberate so that our common humanity might point the wounded to Him who "is able to do immeasurably more than all we can ask or imagine." On the eve of His own greatest ordeal, Jesus told His disciples, "apart from Me you can do nothing." Christ in us has turned our deficits into our greatest advantage.

In our Great Inadequacy, we shine as living beacons illuminating the Answer to all evil and suffering. It is Him—in us, and *for* them. We are not gods, nor are we required to fix the problem. When we understand these things, the cure can flow freely between the hurting and the God of all Comfort.

But there is a warning sign posted here. Knowing our limitations can be a minefield of temptation, marked by the pride of our own humility. It is a nearly undetectable toxin, a leisurely hearing loss to the voice of the Holy Spirit, who faithfully whispers in our ear, "Thou art only a man"; it slips in as a painless blurring, a cataract that subtly blinds us to the illusion of our own indispensability.

Hurting people do not need more earthliness. That is what got them into their situation. Neither do they need a visit from another casualty of pride. They want transcendence, something that flows not from an abundance of training as much as it does from our own human frailties fused with an unadulterated reliance on God. This is the essence of meekness, and we carry with us the benefits of a kingdom and a King from another world.

"Think of the power that will fit us for all crises," Alexander MacLaren wrote, "With the power of Jesus in our spirits we shall never have to attempt a duty for which we are not strengthened, nor to front a danger from (and in which) He will not defend us. With His life in us we shall be ready for the long hours of uneventful, unexciting duties, and for the short spurts that make exacting calls on us. We 'shall run and not be weary; we shall walk and not faint.' If we live in Jesus we shall always be in 'a land of peace,' and no 'plague shall come nigh our dwelling.' Even when the soles of our feet rest in the waters of Jordan, the waters of Jordan shall be cut off, and we shall pass over on dry ground into the land of peace, where they that would swallow us up shall be far away for ever."[lxxxi]

How well the Apostle Paul understood this, as he reminded the whole world—as He reminded us—of God's great purpose for all our inadequacies:

"Praise be to the God and Father of our Lord Jesus Christ, the Father of compassion and the God of all comfort, who comforts us in all our troubles, so that we can comfort those in any trouble with the comfort we ourselves have received from God. For just as the sufferings of Christ flow over into our lives, so also through Christ our comfort overflows. If we are distressed, it is for your comfort and salvation; if we are comforted, it is for your comfort, which produces in you patient endurance of the same sufferings we suffer. And our hope for you is firm, because we know that just as you share in our sufferings, so also you share in our comfort."[lxxxii]

Irish missionary Amy Carmichael also understood. After a bad fall that left her bedridden for much of the rest of her life, she wrote:

Hast thou no scar?

No hidden scar on foot or side or hand

I hear thee sung as mighty in the land,

I hear them hail thy bright ascendant star;

Hast thou no scar?

Hast thou no wound?

Yet, I was wounded by the archers, spent.

Leaned Me against the tree to die, and rent

By ravening beasts that compassed Me, I swooned;

Hast thou no wound?

No wound? No scar?

Yes, as the Master shall the servant be,

And pierced are the feet that follow Me;

But thine are whole.

Can he have followed far

Who has no wound? No scar?[lxxxiii]

"PIE"

"Pie."

—A Chaplaincy code word for "I need to talk"

We caught each other's eyes and paused. Sirens. Nearby. No eating, no talking, just listening past the incessant café noise. The wailing faded beneath the din and my colleagues and I, uniformed and fresh from a training event, guessed—*hoped*—it was just an ambulance racing someone to a nearby hospital.

The mood of our meal became guarded as we pulled phones from our pockets and set them face-up on the table—just in case.

One of them rang.

"Fatality accident—motorcycle versus SUV, the deputies on scene are requesting Chaplains." A minivan made an illegal turn in front of an oncoming road-rocket, killing the cyclist and traumatizing the uninjured occupants of the van.

Dinner was done. The scene was half a block from the restaurant, and we arrived in minutes and went to work. The investigators concluded that a young man returning home from work on his motorcycle—driving the speed limit and wearing his helmet—was cut off when a van turned left in front of him.

Another tragedy, but no more so than the last one, I thought. Pretty routine, I thought. Someone will now call an on-duty Chaplain to do the death notification, I thought. But the deputy thought differently. Like all cops, he hated making death notifications.

"Chaplain, can you help me with this?" he asked.

"No problem," I said, but I wasn't so sure…

Knock, knock, knock.

The door opened to a smiling, shirtless, middle-aged man. Then he noticed the uniforms.

"Uh oh." His eyes widened and his face dropped. He awakened his wife, the mother of the young victim, and we walked through the notification procedure and destroyed their lives. Sad, but routine, I thought.

Then, amidst the sobbing and wailing, we learned about the son. He had just come home to his parents from combat duty in Afghanistan. He was a hero.

And then we learned about his mom. She was the mother of two sons, the oldest of whom was killed in a vehicle accident years earlier. The younger son was her sole-surviving child, and now he, too was gone.

And today was her birthday.

Not routine, not ever. All tragedy maims the heart and leaves deep scars—even on seasoned professionals. It became the most painful notification I ever made. The unanticipated level of tragedy I delivered to this sweet woman all but ended my Chaplaincy career. I still bleed from it.

Which is why God invented pie.

Let me explain…

It can become your own private pandemic, a very real possibility that many are unwilling to admit lest they risk appearing less than a superhero. The anguish of others is contagious. It is subtle and virulent, and none of us, neither saint nor Superman, are immune to the infectious nature of another's tragedy.

As we minister to traumatized people, direct exposure to emotional intensity, graphic accounts of an event, or the horrific nature of a scene can expose us to a toxic dose of emotional transference. Compassion fatigue, anxiety, empathetic overload or even burnout can, over time, overwhelm even the most seasoned caregivers as they attend to those suffering dreadful circumstances. And it is especially catching if the crisis becomes mutual.

Jack Herrmann, volunteer mental health lead for the American Red Cross in New York, warns counselors to be alert to the fact that they are not immune to the effects of trauma in others. "Most mental health professionals get into the business to help others, but they do so at some peril to themselves. Sustained efforts to support others through crisis can place counselors at risk of vicarious traumatization, which can cause them to experience the same anxieties as victims, such as sleeplessness, nightmares, mood changes, or changes in interest levels."[lxxxiv]

His warning is well founded, but there is a problem, not with the warning, but with spiritual presumption. Clinicians do not usually validate the idea of functional evil and typically ignore such "psychological" red flags. But a person of faith may unwisely believe that he is impervious to such effects: he "has the Lord" with him, and he will go and pray and everything will be all right in the morning. This can be an unfortunate assumption, because even though a Christian caregiver may hugely benefit from his new nature in Christ, he still lives in an unredeemed body that is subject to (among other things) intense emotional distress. Add to this his almost daily and disproportionate exposure to the evils of this world and somewhere down the road there are bound to be problems.

Placer County Law Enforcement Chaplaincy in California wisely recognized this vulnerability as a major threat to the well-being and ministry capacity of its chaplains, and they took action. To reduce the risk of contagious trauma, they invented a code word, "pie," meaning, "I have been on a difficult call-out and I need to talk." Then the chaplain meets with one of his colleagues for pie and coffee, and in the course of bearing each other's burdens, they usually eat or drink neither.

But the one who believes they have to muscle their way through the heartache of another's trauma because, "I am a minister and a Christian, and such things should not affect me—after all, I was not the victim; I am the helper,"—he has already become a casualty. His lifeboat has become filled with victims *and* their abundant baggage; now there is no more room for its captain. And the boat is beginning to sink.

Time for pie...

"Even in our sleep, pain, which cannot forget, falls drop by drop upon the heart until, in our own despair, against our will, comes wisdom through the awful grace of God."

— Aeschylus

SELECTED BIBLIOGRAPHY & END NOTES

- Aikman, David, *The Delusion of Disbelief*. Illinois: Salt River, an imprint of Tyndale House Publishers, Inc., 2008

- Carus, Paul, *The Gospel of Buddha*. Chicago: The Open Court Publishing Co., 1894

- *Collected Essays*. New York: Bantam Books, published by arrangement with Harper and Row, Publishers, Inc., 1964

- Dawkins, Richard, *The God Delusion*. New York: Houghton Mifflin Company, 2008

- *Encyclopedia of Religion*. MacMillan Reference Books, 2005

- *Essays Presented to Charles Williams*. Edited by C. S. Lewis; Grand Rapids MI.: Eerdman's Publishing, 1978

- Frankl, Viktor, *Man's Search for Meaning*. New York: Pocket Books, 1985

- Freud, Sigmund, *Civilization and Its Discontents*. New York: W.W. Norton, 2005

- Freud, Sigmund, *The Future of an Illusion*. Translated by James Strachey. London: Hogarth Press, 1968

- Gaita, Raimond, *A Common Humanity: Thinking About Love and Truth and Justice*. New York: Routledge, 2002

- Geisler, Norman L., *The Baker Encyclopedia of Christian Apologetics*. Grand Rapids, MI.: Baker Books, 1999

- Geisler, Norman L., Brooks, Ronald M., *When Skeptics Ask*. Wheaton, Il.: Victor Books, 1990

- Guinness, Os, *Time for Truth: Living Free in a World of Lies, Hype, and Spin*. Grand Rapids, MI.: Baker Books, 2000

- Guinness, Os, *Unspeakable*. New York: HarperCollins Publishers, Inc., 2005

- Huxley, Aldous, *Collected Essays*. New York: Bantam Books, published with Harper & Row, Publishers, Inc., 1964

- *Hindu Scriptures*. R.C. Zaehner, editor and translation. New York: Alfred A. Knopf, 1992

- *The Holy Bible, New International Version*. Grand Rapids, MI: Zondervan, 1978

- Kreeft, Dr. Peter John, *Making Sense Out of Suffering*. Cincinnati, OH.: St. Anthony Messenger Press, 1986

- Krishnamurthy, V., *Gems from the Ocean of Hindu Thought Vision and Practice*. 2004

- Levy, Primo, *If This is a Man*, London: Abacus, 1897

- Levy, Primo, *Survival at Auschwitz*. New York: Touchstone, 1996

- Lewis, Clive Staples, *Mere Christianity*. Westwood, NJ.: Barbour and Company, 1952

- Lewis, Clive Staples, *The Problem of Pain*. New York: Collier Books, 1962

- Lewis, Clive Staples, *The Screwtape Letters, with Screwtape Proposes a Toast*. Revised Edition. New York: Collier Books, 1982

- MacLaren, Alexander, *Exposition of Holy Scripture: Isaiah and Jeremiah*. BiblioBazaar, 2006

- *The Meditations of Marcus Aurelius Antoninus*. R.B. Rutherford, Translator. New York: Oxford University Press, 2008

- *Modern Essays*. Compiled by Christopher Morley. University of Michigan: Harcourt, Brace & Company, 1921

- Newell, William R., *Romans Verse by Verse*. Chicago, Il.: Moody Press, 1938

- Nicholi, Armand M., *The Question of God*. New York: The Free Press, 2002

- Nietzsche, Friedrich, *The Twilight of the Idols and The Anti-Christ: or How to Philosophize with a Hammer*. New York: Penguin Putnam, Inc., 1990

- Perry, Michael J., *Toward a Theory of Human Rights: Religion, Law, Courts*. Cambridge University Press, 2007

- Piper, John, *Don't Waste Your Life*. Wheaton, Il.: Crossway Books, 2004

- Sagan, Carl, *Billions and Billions: Thoughts on Life and Death at the Brink of the Millennium*. New York: Ballantine Books, 1997

- Russell, Bertrand, *A Free Man's Worship and other Essays*. London: Unwin Books, 1976

- Sagan, Carl, *Cosmos*. New York: Ballantine Books, 1985

- Sayadaw, Ven. Mahasi, *Basic Buddhism*. Buddha Dharma Education Association and BuddhaNet, 2008

- Solzhenitsyn, Alexander, *The Gulag Archipelago, 1918-1956*. New York: Harper & Row, 1985

- Solzhenitsyn, Alexander, *A World Split Apart*. Bookyards Library to the World, 1978

- Strobel, Lee, *The Case for Christ*. Grand Rapids, MI.: Zondervan, 1998

- *The Western Book of the Dead*. Inter-Varsity Press, Downers Grove, Illinois, 1970

- Vine, W.E.; Unger, Merril F.; White, William, *Vine's Complete Expository of Old and New Testament Words*. Chattanooga, TN: AMG Publishers; Abridged edition, 1998

- Weil, Simone, *Gravity and Grace*. London: Routledge, 1995

- Wilder-Smith, A.E., *Let Us Reason*. Costa Mesa, CA.: The Word for Today, 2007

- Zacharias, Ravi, *The Lotus and the Cross*. Colorado Springs, CO.: Multnomah Books, 2001

[i] C.S. Lewis, *The Case for Christianity*

[ii] Sigmund Freud, *The Future of an Illusion*. Translated by James Strachey. London: Hogarth Press, 1968

[iii] Sigmund Freud, *Civilization and Its Discontents*. New York: W.W. Norton, 2005

[iv] Primo Levy, *If This is a Man*, London: Abacus, 1897

[v] Os Guinness, *Unspeakable*. New York: HarperCollins Publishers, Inc., 2005, p.109

[vi] Os Guinness, *Long Journey Home: A Guide To Your Search for the Meaning in Life*. Colorado Springs, CO: WaterBrook Press, 2001

[vii] *The Gospel of Buddha*, told by Paul Carus. Chicago: The Open Court Publishing Co., 1894, p.13

[viii] Guinness, Os, *Unspeakable*. New York: HarperCollins Publishers, Inc., 2005, p.121

[ix] V. Krishnamurthy, *Gens from the Ocean of Hindu Thought, Vision, and Practice*, Beach 11: Live Happily, The Gita Way, Chapter 6: MAyA, The First Secret of Secrets, , Jan.19, 2004

[x] *Maya* (Illusion), from Wikipedia.com

[xi] R.C.Zaehner, editor and translation, 1992. *Hindu Scriptures*. New York: Alfred A. Knopf

[xii] Os Guinness, *Unspeakable*. New York: HarperCollins Publishers, Inc., 2005, p.200

[xiii] Ven. Mahasi Sayadaw, *Basic Buddhism*, "The Theory of Karma." Buddha Dharma Education Association and BuddhaNet

[xiv] Ibid.

[xv] Ibid.

[xvi] Dr. Peter Kreeft, from a lecture, "*The Dark Side: Shining light on three kinds of evil: suffering, death and sin.*" Socrates in the City, New York, NY. May 4, 2005

[xvii] Os Guinness, *Unspeakable*. New York: HarperCollins Publishers, Inc., 2005, p.119

[xviii] Seneca, Roman Stoic philosopher (c. 4 BCE—CE 65)

[xix] Marcus Aurelius, *Meditations*

[xx] Bill Allin, *Turning It Around*. http://billallin.com

[xxi] Mark Twain, *Which Was the Dream?*

[xxii] Epicurus, Translated by Robert Drew Hicks http://www.epicurus.net/en/menoeceus.html

[xxiii] Garth Kemerling, *Philosophy Pages*, Philosophical Dictionary: http://www.philosophypages.com/dy/e9.htm#evil

xxiv Ibid.

xxv Carl Sagan, *Cosmos*. New York: Ballantine Books, 1985

xxvi Carl Sagan, quoted from John Stear, *No Answers in Genesis*

xxvii Ann Druyan, Epilogue to *Billions and Billions: Thoughts on Life and Death at the Brink of the Millennium.* New York: Ballantine Books, 1997

xxviii Dr. A.E. Wilder-Smith, *Let Us Reason.* Costa Mesa, CA.: The Word for Today, 2007, p.105

xxix Guinness, Os, *Unspeakable.* New York: HarperCollins Publishers, Inc., 2005, p.131

xxx Alexander Solzhenitsyn, *A World Aflame.* From an address given at Harvard University. Bookyards Library to the World, 1978, p.6

xxxi Ibid., p.9

xxxii Michael J. Perry, *Toward a Theory of Human Rights: Religion, Law, Courts.* Excerpt. Cambridge University Press

xxxiii Ibid.

xxxiv Richard Dawkins, *The God Delusion.* New York: Houghton Mifflin Company, 2008, p.31

xxxv *Encyclopedia of Religion.* MacMillan Reference Books, 2005

xxxvi Sam Harris, *Letter to a Christian Nation.* New York, Alfred A. Knopf, 2006, p.23-24

xxxvii Simone Weil, *Gravity and Grace, Illusions.* London, Routledge, 1995, p.105

xxxviii Adherents.com, http://www.adherents.com/Religions_By_Adherents.html

xxxix Clarence Darrow, cited in Smithsonian Magazine, *Criminal Minds*, August 2008, p.75

xl Guinness, Os, *Unspeakable.* New York: HarperCollins Publishers, Inc., 2005, p.110

xli Aldous Huxley, from "D.H. Lawrence," *Collected Essays*, Bantam Books, published by arrangement with Harper and Row, Publishers, Inc., March 1964

xlii C.S. Lewis, *The Screwtape Letters, with Screwtape Proposes a Toast.* Revised Edition. New York: Collier Books, 1982, p.16

xliii C.S. Lewis, *Mere Christianity.* Westwood, NJ.: Barbour and Company, 1952, p.68

xliv Friedrich Nietzsche, *Twilight of the Idols.* 1888 (from a phrase originally coined by Goethe)

xlv *The Western Book of the Dead, XI*, Inter-Varsity Press, Downers Grove, Illinois, 1970 xlvi Rom 2:15

xlvii Alexander Solzhenitsyn, *The Gulag Archipelago, 1918-1956*. New York: Harper & Row, 1985

xlviii C.S. Lewis, *Mere Christianity*. Westwood, NJ.: Barbour and Company, 1952, p.23

xlix Guinness, Os, *Unspeakable*. New York: HarperCollins Publishers, Inc., 2005

l Rom 1:18-23

li Rom 1:24-32

lii James Anderson, *Evidential Faith: Understanding Pentecostal Theology: The Problem of Evil.*

liii Dr. Peter John Kreeft, as cited by Lee Strobel, *The Case for Christ*. Grand Rapids, MI.: Zondervan, 1998

liv Norman L. Geisler and Ronald M. Brooks. *When Skeptics Ask*, Wheaton, Il.: Victor Books, 1990

lv Time Warner Cable Customer Handbook, Desert Cities, 2008

lvi Dr. Peter John Kreeft, *Making Sense Out of Suffering*, Cincinnati: St. Anthony Messenger Press, 1986, p. 93.

lvii *Os Guinness Looks Evil in the Eye*. From an interview by Interview by Stan Guthrie March 10, 2005, VirtueOnLine.org

lviii Roy Hattersley, "Faith does breed charity: We atheists have to accept that most believers are better human beings," *The Guardian*, 12 September, 2005; cited by David Aikman, *The Delusion of Disbelief*, Salt River, an imprint of Tyndale House Publishers, Inc., Illinois, 2008, p.97

lix Friedrich Nietzsche, *Human, All-too-Human,* 1878

lx Ravi Zacharias, *The Lotus and the Cross*. Audio Book. Colorado Springs, CO.: Multnomah Books, 2001

lxi Dr. Peter John Kreeft, *Making Sense Out of Suffering* Cincinnati: St. Anthony Messenger Press, 1986, p.16.

lxii Ibid., p. 58-59

lxiii Os Guinness, *Time for Truth: Living Free in a World of Lies, Hype, and Spin*. Grand Rapids, MI.: Baker Books, 2000

lxiv Gene Roddenberry, cited in Time Magazine, April 1988, Text copyright 1988 by Gene Roddenberry

lxv Suggested by the Steve Turner poem *Creed*, excerpted from Ravi Zacharias' book *Can Man Live Without God?* Pages 42-44

lxvi C.S. Lewis, *Mere Christianity*. Westwood, NJ.: Barbour and Company, 1952, p.25

lxvii John 11:32-35

lxviii Os Guinness, *Unspeakable*. New York: HarperCollins Publishers, Inc., 2005, p. 144

lxix Ibid., p.145

lxx C.S. Lewis, *The Problem of Pain*, Harper Collins Edition 2001

lxxi Romans 1:18-32

lxxii John 9:2-3

lxxiii Luke 13:4-5a

lxxiv Simone Weil, *Gravity and Grace*, London, Routledge, 1995, p. 73

lxxv Daniel 3:16b-18

lxxvi Attributed to Viktor Frankl

lxxvii Michael Horton, *James Montgomery Boice: Servant of the Word*; *Modern Reformation*, 9 no. 5 (September/October 2000): 10-1

lxxviii Simone Weil, *Gravity and Grace*, London, Routledge, 1995, p. 102)

lxxix Os Guinness, *Riding the Storm*. From a lecture presented at the C.S. Lewis Institute, August 2001

lxxx Romans 8:31-39

lxxxi Alexander MacLaren, *Exposition of Holy Scripture: Isaiah and Jeremiah*; *Calms and Cries*. BiblioBazaar, 2006

lxxxii 2 Corinthians 1:3-7

lxxxiii Amy Beatrice Carmichael, *Hast Thou No Scar?* From *Toward Jerusalem* by Amy Carmichael, Society for Promotion of Christian Knowledge, London

lxxxiv The Warner Graduate School of Education and Human Development at the University of Rochester, *Counselors Combat Disaster for Students, Themselves*, The Warner School website article, "News and Events," http://www.rochester.edu/Warner/newsevents/warnereducator/spring02/counselors.html

Made in the USA
Middletown, DE
29 May 2022

66372083R00086